BROKEN OR BEAUTIFUL

The Struggle of Modern Dressage

BY DOMINIQUE BARBIER AND LIZ CONROD

First published in 2021 by
Xenophon Press
Franktown, Virginia 23354
XenophonPress@gmail.com

Copyright 2021 Dominique Barbier and Liz Conrod

All rights reserved. No part of this book may be reproduced, by any means, with written permission from the publisher, except by a reviewer quoting brief excerpts for a review in a magazine, newspaper or website. Credit should be given to the publisher in all review articles referencing the website: www.XenophonPress.com without exception.

Disclaimer of Liability

The authors and publisher shall have neither liability nor responsibility to any person or entity with respect to any loss or damage caused or alleged to be caused directly or indirectly by the information contained in this book. While the book is as accurate as the authors can make it, there may be errors omissions, and inaccuracies.

Xenophon Press encourages the use of approved safety helmets in
all equestrian sports and activities.

ISBN: 9781948717281

Cover Photos:
Left: Anonymous
Right: Ultraje VO Owned by Melinda d'Amico Photo by Candida von Braun

BROKEN OR BEAUTIFUL
The Struggle of Modern Dressage

BY DOMINIQUE BARBIER AND LIZ CONROD

With an Introduction by
Dorota Raciborska, Ph. D.

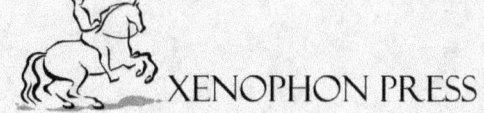

DEDICATIONS

To my Dad who believed in my early days' dedication.
To all my students and riders who share my passion in looking deeper in the horses and themselves.
I would like to thank my wife Debra, who helped me develop the process.
And to my friend Liz Conrod, without whom the book would not have been possible.
—Dominique Barbier

To my Mom, Vera Conrod, from whom I first learned to be compassionate.
To my husband, Tom Ancona, without whom this life would not be possible.
To Dominique, who has been my *Mestre* and to whom I am eternally grateful for
the knowledge and direction of my riding career.
—Liz Conrod

ACKNOWLEDGEMENTS

We would like to thank Richard Williams of Xenophon Press for his ongoing enthusiasm for publishing in the tradition of Ivan Bezugloff, the original creator of Dressage & CT magazine and Xenophon Press.

Xenophon Press has remained dedicated to publishing work that promotes Classical knowledge and the welfare of horses.

The authors would like to especially acknowledge researcher extraordinaire, Jane Otto of Flemington, New Jersey. Jane contributed immensely to our work by obtaining copies of expired F. E. I. rules.

We are also grateful for the Introduction contributed by Dorota Raciborska, PhD. Certified Equine-Facilitated Human Development. Quito, Ecuador

Thank you to Sarah Richter who helped so much with photo editing.

Thank you to Keron Psillas for her contribution of photos and editing.

—Dominique & Liz

PUBLISHER'S FOREWORD

As I embark on my tenth year as publisher/editor at Xenophon Press I can hardly believe the two walls of books behind and beside me that we have had the privilege of working on over the past decade. I met Ivan Bezugloff in 1984 at the Los Angeles Olympics when I was a 'on assignment' as a photographer in the warmup arena for his magazine Dressage and Combined Training (Dressage & CT). Later, I met Ivan in 1986 at the World Dressage Championships in Cedar Valley. I was thoroughly impressed by his magazine, and regularly devoured every page of every article. Decades later, when Ivan had been wholesaling books to me, and he started to slow down, and asked me to take over for him at Xenophon Press, I was both honored and daunted. He graciously mentored me in the publishing process until his final days. He inspired many professionals, created chances and opportunities for professionals and allowed differing voices to be heard in the dressage world.

I began my life in America in California, not far from where Dominique Barbier finally settled but ironically our paths did not cross much until I moved to the east coast. Many of our authors were the disciples of Nuno Oliveira and the French School of which Dominique was clearly a part. So our discussions over the phone, sharing contacts, opinions, trading books kept us in regular contact.

1984 marked the beginning of my watching international competition and I have attended CDIs for decades ever since. With increasing suspicion about the direction of competitive dressage, I was growing weary of what I was seeing and of what was being rewarded in competition especially in contrast to what I had been taught, and what our authors were writing about.

Dominique and Liz's essay is a much needed confrontation of the direct problem that we face with 'dressage today.' Exactly what do we mean by 'dressage'? and do we mean to give dressage a bad name? Even innocent on-lookers can discern a tense, stressed horse versus one in relaxation and lightness. Correct training and principles must prevail over mechanization. I believe this is a very necessary 'Red book' that should call all of us to arms in a peaceful way to practice our very best way of being horse-people first with our own horses, and then through activism in the horse community at large.

Only through education can we make change for the better. Dominique and Liz ask important questions and, like any good riding lesson, they repeat themselves, and say the same thing over again in many different ways, knowing that their message will eventually be heard and understood through repetition. Just as they repeat themselves, so must we speak up repeatedly to the officials, the F. E. I. the stewards, competitors, judges and trainers.

Dominique and Liz's book joins an ever-growing list of educational materials available in the Xenophon Press Library listed at the back of this book. We are constantly adding to this list for the betterment of the art and the sport of classical equitation.

We hope this book inspires you to take action on behalf of the horse.

—Richard Williams
Publisher/Editor-in-Chief
Xenophon Press

INTRODUCTION

On a typical sunny morning I held the reins with the tips of my fingers, with only the weight of the leather between my hands and the mare's mouth. As I rebalanced my center of gravity towards her hindquarters, I felt her back rise softly and her energy focus. She was interpreting my intention and responding with specific direction and speed of motion. Just the tipping of my fingers was enough to signal to her to incline her neck further, and a turn of my head indicated to her a change in direction. While accompanying the shifts of my shoulders altering the angle of our movement still proved a challenge for her, it will only be a matter of time before we will be able to move in unison in all directions.

This way of riding requires little physical effort, but it does require understanding and a deeper awareness. The prize, the lightness and ease of motion, as well as the disarming partnership with the horse, is more than worth the effort. In fact, there is no better feeling in the world for both the rider _and_ the horse. This feeling, I believe, is why horses, through an unknown and ancient process, have consented to accompany and serve humans on our evolutionary path. This is also why working with horses becomes a developmental journey for both beings involved.

To ride/train/judge in ignorance of this phenomenon of lightness and power generously laid at the human's feet, or to trade it and equine welfare for material trappings, is a travesty. The book you hold in your hands bravely shows how many of us have either lost sight of this ultimate goal of human-equine relationship, or have never found it. The whites of the eyes flashing, wringing tail, resistance to using his body in certain ways—all these indicate that our actions do not feel good to the horse. He can only speak with his body, and any resistance simply means 'no.' What will it take for people to take note, hear this "no," and act upon it with benevolence and empathy?

This book rings the urgently needed alarm, and gives voice to the growing frustration, dismay, and even desperation of horse-men and -women who see the suffering and the damage inflicted, and the lost great opportunity. It lays out clearly and with photographic evidence, the contradiction between the set of rules established to protect the welfare of the horse, and the damning actions we commonly observe in competition arenas. One by one the F. E. I. articles for Dressage competition are examined, and the misunderstandings, omissions, and failure to enforce them are unpacked. This brief volume makes totally null and void the excuse of ignorance.

At the moment, the majority of equestrians are oblivious to the suffering they cause, and to the quality of relationship which the sentience of the horse makes possible. Of those who have noticed the dreadful abuse and distancing from the ethos of dressage over the past decades, some have decided to do no harm by not competing, by riding bit-less, treeless, or not riding at all. However, in this way, by failing to provide him with the opportunity to reach his full potential as a supremely physical and athletic being, they risk abandoning the horse. May this very accessible book open the eyes of the public to the cruelty exhibited, dispel the illusion among the equestrian community that inflicting pain on horses is in any way justifiable, and provide the food for thought and the encouragement to young and old students of the horse to delve deeper, read and study the old masters and comprehend the opportunity they are offered.

It is a great honor to have been asked to write an introduction to Dominique and Liz's book. As a life-long student of the horse, and of human development, my true awakening to the way it is possible to relate to the horse and to ride occurred after Colonel Wickert of the Brazilian cavalry, introduced me to Dominique Barbier's *Dressage for the New Age*. It spoke of new and exciting possibilities for riding and put in question everything I had been taught about equitation in the preceding 40 years. It begs the question as to why the very old knowledge about the art of equitation has been limited to the few. Perhaps in the age of scientific advancement such knowledge appears too esoteric; or maybe, keeping these secrets well-guarded may have helped ensure success for the few in a very competitive field. It is about time that this knowledge be widely discussed and taught, for the benefit of the horse and ultimately for the benefit of humanity.

—Dorota Raciborska, Ph. D.
Certified Equine-Facilitated
Human Development
Quito, Ecuador

"It is rare to see a rider who is truly passionate about the horse and his training taking a profound interest in Dressage with self-abnegation and making this extraordinary subtle work one of the dominant motivations of his life."
—Mestre Nuno Oliveira

*Azulejos of Marques de Marialva from Quinta do Brejo.
The Classical Principles are the very basis of the F. E. I. rules*

DOMINIQUE BARBIER AND LIZ CONROD

MESTRE NUNO OLIVEIRA

> "Equestrian art is the perfect understanding
> between the rider and his horse."
> —Mestre Nuno Olivera's book *Reflections on Equestrian Art*.

Classical correct extended trot. The frame of the horse corresponds to the length of the stride, as prescribed in the F. E. I. Rules. Dom Fransisco, Utah Bred Thoroughbred ridden by Dominique Barbier. Photo by Marcia Hart

INTRODUCTION

The premise of this book is to give the reader a fair evaluation of the riding in the world today. We are writing now because the state of Dressage and other equine sports is not respectful to the welfare of horses. We mean to explain why we say this, and when, why and how this negative trend has come about.

Please forgive us, some of our language is strong, and needs to be, in order to defend and speak for the horses. The purpose of this effort is to empower other people who are concerned as well. We hope to encourage people to evaluate, think, and to speak out. Horses are meant to be our partners, not a means to an end for financial gain nor for gaining power in the sport.

It is important that people are well informed in order to explain why long-established principles are to be treasured and preserved. In the modern electronic and super-fast paced world, people are and feel disconnected from nature and themselves. This has helped lead to looking at horses as little more than vehicles.

We are in an era in which each individual must decide why they ride, how they train and how they will treat their horses.

Horses are here, in fact, to help us achieve a higher level of understanding. Over forty years ago Dominique Barbier wrote *Dressage for the New Age* to help people to understand that horses are much more than most people thought. The emphasis on mental communication and visualization helped many people to see a bigger picture of horses and their riding. After the books *Meditation for Two* and *The Alchemy of Lightness* were published, we had a chance to better understand what "Lightness for Enlightenment" ™ means.

We feel that time is of the essence and it is imperative that we pause now, to reevaluate the direction of riding, most especially Dressage, worldwide.

We are at a true crossroads. If we do not alter the culture of the competitive horse show world, we are at risk of losing and forgetting what Dressage is all about. We have a new generation of trainers, judges and riders coming up and with the loss of most classical training, philosophies and ethics, this could very well lead to a loss of Equestrian Art.

Hopefully the great schools of the world can reassert their role in education. With the help of some individuals we have chance to keep the principles of Communication, Harmony, and Lightness alive.

Knowledge that is not practiced is very easily lost. While certainly not all of historical practices are of value, we need to study the Masters that came before us. Horses have not become modern. Trots have not changed. When todays trainers and judges speak of modern Dressage, they, without knowing it, disrespect the art, history and the horse.

We have a rich legacy of knowledge from past Masters to draw from. As well, the F. E. I. founders left us with excellent guidelines for how to compete with our horses without compromising their well-being.

What is happening today, is that "modern" ideas and values are in practice that are detrimental, hurtful to horses.

In the following pages you will read the words Lightness, Harmony, Balance, Relaxation over and over again. This is because the attitude of training with these ideals in mind are what Dressage is all about. It is what F. E. I. founders were most concerned with preserving.

This legacy is being squandered. When we disregard the wisdom and knowledge, we betray our horses. We must honor the legacy, not ignore it. F. E. I. founders left us with appropriate words, ideas, principles to follow. We must return to that path.

Happy horse in balance with energy. "Position - No Action" beautifully demonstrated. Xavante ridden by Dominique Barbier. Photo by Sarah Richter

CHAPTER 1:
THE HAPPY ATHLETE

F. E. I. ARTICLE 401: OBJECT AND GENERAL PRINCIPLES OF DRESSAGE States:
*"The object of Dressage is the development of the Horse
into a happy Athlete through harmonious education."*

This is an important foundational principle of Dressage training and should be a foundational principle of Dressage Competition as well.

Dressage is to develop the happy athlete. It is a relationship which allows the horse to be in comfortable positions with relaxation and suppleness. The athlete can and should be developed in harmony.

With the communication of the Mind, meaning being totally present, and visualizing, we can understand the horse better. When we use our mind to communicate with our horse, we can begin to have a conversation with our horse. In this way we can start to understand what he is saying to us and we can better help him to understand what we are saying to him. It helps him to understand what we want and be happy with us. This is what communicating with a horse is about. It is where the gifts come from, for horse and rider.

Beliefs and attitude of rider will guide the training of the horse.

We believe that the horse who is in a good physical and mental position, will stay in that state, if he has the proper energy and he is not disturbed.

"Energy, as we know, is a constant flow of the river."
—Dominique Barbier.

We do not need to use our legs to produce energy, in fact constant and heavy use of legs disturbs the horse.

We further believe that using the hands for direction and control disturbs the horse. Let us remind you that the position of the hands with the proper length of the rein is there only to position the horses head, and neck, what we call in French the "*Ramener.*"

The complete relaxation of the rider and the ability to move with the horse will help the horse's mental attitude.

When we are aware of being the leader of the dance, we need to know the dance and to stay present in the dance.

If these beliefs are not understood or recognized, then most riders will resort to force and physical demands on their partner, as they have no idea that any alternative exists. Sadly then, the very relationship that they are seeking is destroyed.

"Elegantly Forcing horses, is still Forcing" Dominique Barbier during a symposium in Bavaria

CLASSICAL DRESSAGE IS AN ART FORM

The F. E. I. mission says it is to preserve classical principles of Dressage. Through the years, the competitive aspect of dressage changed this focus. The F. E. I. definition of a happy supple athlete reminds us of the mental and the physical nature of the relationship, which is not seen in the competitive ring much anymore.

Competition is not fostering these principles.

Dressage is a simple progression through understanding, to achieve a rewarding experience for both partners leading to beauty. Dressage is ART. It is very rare to see the horse happy in the competition ring.

It is an art form that involves two partners, horse and rider, and both deserve to be comfortable. Both partners should be happy to dance together.

Dressage should always be in the horse's best interests, physically and mentally.

Communication can be both physical and mental, when two beings communicate truly, they are in harmony. We all seek (or claim to seek) a connection with our horses, a joy in sharing time and understanding of one another, real communication. Real dancing.

When the army and the world stopped using horses for practical purposes, their lives changed. Horses had a daily purpose, farming, transportation, etc. and were part of everyday life. They had to be healthy for doing their job. Their well-being was primordial. Horses worked long hours, then rested in standing stalls only, waiting for the next day of work.

Then horses became objects of luxury and entertainment. A lot of horse and human relationships disappeared and most people lost contact with horses in everyday life. They lost the skill and knowledge of how to be with them and to communicate with them. Training became more specific and now more sport focused, Dressage, Three Day Eventing and Jumping etc.

The first modern Olympic Games were held in 1896, and the first equestrian events were held in 1912. Historically, Dressage equestrians were either military personnel, royalty or privileged wealthy individuals. They were the only people allowed to compete as they had the Amateur status required.

The addition of equestrian events in Olympic games led to the formation of Federation Equestre Internationale (F. E. I.) in 1921, for the express purpose of protecting the welfare of horses now participating in equestrian games. They did this by using prescribed rules for competitors used as guidelines.

The Classical Principles are the foundation for these rules.

The original rules of F. E. I. allowed that trainers with different methods (predominately French and German) could compete together. They wanted to be certain that whichever school competitors subscribed to, that the welfare of the horse was always preserved, and that the horses would be judged by a Classical (universal) criteria.

Today Dressage is often thought of only in terms of competition; all the way from local schooling shows to what is now considered the ultimate; the Olympic Games. Dressage is not competition!

Dressage is the art of training, to educate horses how best to carry a rider, with ease, finesse and lightness. It is true that this method was used to make a horse more useful in war, bull fighting and to carry the King in comfort. Riders could concentrate on slaying an enemy or a bull if his horse was balanced, could turn quickly and easily, and responded the quickest and lightest of aids so the rider could concentrate on the task at hand.

When we search the internet today, we find varying definitions.

Webster says it is "a SPORT involving the execution of precise movements by a trained horse in response to barely perceptible signals from its rider." Webster does acknowledge that the word stems from the French word meaning 'training'

Oxford says 'The ART of riding and training a horse in a manner that develops obedience, flexibility and balance."

Wikipedia says 'a highly skilled form of riding performed in exhibition and competition, as well as an Art sometimes pursued solely for the sake of mastery'.

In today's world, we think it safe to say that competitive dressage is what the vast majority of people think encompasses what "Dressage" means.

There are most certainly many people that ride and train their horse using dressage principles that will never enter a show ring, and indeed we believe more and more such people, as the competitive dressage world is becoming less and less about the horses training and welfare, and looks more and more distasteful.

CHAPTER 2:
EVOLUTION

In researching the original rules of the F. E. I., Dominique realized how fortunate he is to have learned from two different classical Masters. Early on, he says, his first teacher was from the Cadre Noir of Saumur, Adjudant-Chef Peyrat. His teacher was first of his promotion (first in his class) in Saumur. He could have chosen any assignment he wished. Instead of staying in Saumur he went to Saint-Cyr Military Academy Coetquident in Britany where four sous-officers were stationed. Every weekend they would compete in racing, three-day eventing (at that time it was called "Military"), jumping and Dressage. They won every event, every time they competed as they had a full and thorough knowledge of all the disciplines.

Dominique's other teacher was *Mestre* Nuno Oliveira.

"My training from these masters involved riding trained horses, and then proceeding with training my own horses. I learned from my experiences and from the horses, the importance of what we term the "Classical principles," by applying them in a practical way. I knew nothing of F. E. I. rules. I was instead, learning how to train, how to ride. This was very different from learning by reading rules and text books. From this background and perspective, I clearly understood why the rules were written as they were."
— Dominique Barbier

The rules are derived from the principles not the other way around. The original F. E. I. rules were written by two horsemen, one French, one German, because these trainers understood and agreed that these rules would protect the horses, beyond school rivalry.

All of these principles are inter-related, and dependent on each other. The Art of Riding is to adjust this ever-evolving puzzle. The process is vitally important, and dynamic, when training your horse is correct. A puzzle cannot have missing pieces and become whole. It has nothing to do with pyramids!

Now that I have trained thousands of horses of all breeds and abilities the following essential rules *always* apply:

> *"The importance of the relaxation of the lower jaw is essential to the whole art of riding."*
> — Dominique Barbier

With this relaxation of the lower jaw, through deglutition we can obtain self-carriage and lightness. This allows us to contemplate *Descente de Main*.

The importance of the Shoulder-In in relaxation which will facilitate the physical, mental and emotional well-being of the horse. The Shoulder-In helps the horse to become more aware of his body, of his balance, and our connection with him. As we will explain in the Shoulder-In chapter, this movement as De La Guérinière said, is the first and last movement we teach the horse. During all of the horses training, the Shoulder-In will be critically important. It will evolve as the horse evolves. It is the most creative movement in the equestrian art. When the F. E. I. changed De la Guérinière's four track Shoulder-In to the three-track Shoulder-In and allowed the angle to be reduced from 45 degrees to 30 degrees, we lost the whole essence of this foundational suppling movement and allowed the rigidity of all the sideways movements.

The importance of attaining the beginning of collection before beginning any lengthening. This is a very essential principle that has been nearly totally forgotten.

The horse needs to have clear awareness of his body before he can expand it into maximizing his movement, in all gaits starting with the walk. You cannot have lengthening and later extension without collection first. A new baby cannot run before he walks.

The importance of the change of frame coming before the change of stride, meaning you need to change the frame before you change the length of the stride, keeping the same balance and lightness. It is very surprising that after all the talk about bio mechanics, this very basic rule is not respected. We see rigid horses in the same frame for all the movements. We even had to invent the terms "leg mover," versus "back mover," because essentially, we do not allow the horse to use his body and his back properly for the movement. When we try to push our horse into a so-called extension without allowing him to lengthen his frame, we handicap him severely. The change of frame is integral to the principle and idea of correct collection.

Shoulder-In in harmony, lightness, partnership. Gabriel ridden by Hilary Klassen. Photo by David Grulke

The importance of the toes touching the ground where they are pointed, eliminating any elevation of the front legs created by contraction, as mentioned in the F. E. I. rules. Ignoring this truth has allowed the ugly 'Spanish Style" trot and bastardized Passage in resistance that we see today. The reason this is so important is that the back of the horse must not be rigid or tight. The true correct extended trot is produced by the back legs reaching under the horse, and matching the front legs. There should be an over stride that is obvious.

Looking at the evolution of the rules definitely explains the complete premeditated deconstruction of the early spirit of the original rules laid out by F. E. I. founders. When the five principles listed above are not adhered to, we arrive at the rigidity and contact which is so pervasive today.

Resistance and rigidity are now used for training instead of the search for lightness through suppleness.

Correct extended trot for a young horse. The toe is pointed to where it will land, as prescribed by the F. E. I. Richmen, Selle Français Stallion ridden by Debra Barbier

The early Olympic games brought together the French and the German schools to compete with each other. People would come together and share their knowledge and practices with each other, by riding tests.

At that time there was no professional 'trainer,' it was the military personnel, and a few "elite" riders riding and training horses. In the Olympic games, all competitors needed to be amateurs. There was no exchange of money for riding or training. The making of money was not a factor in any way.

So, something that was friendly and with an idea of sharing practices and ideas, became a multi-billion-dollar industry and with no thought to friendliness or relationship with your horse.

The body of governance of competitive dressage today is the Federation Equestre Internationale or F. E. I.

Article 401 of the F. E. I. states: "The object of Dressage is the development of the Horse into a HAPPY ATHLETE through harmonious education. As a result, it (the training) makes the horse calm, supple, loose, flexible but ALSO confident, attentive and keen, thus achieving perfect UNDERSTANDING with the Athlete."

Circa 400 B. C., Xenophon was the first person to speak about being nice to the horse, and riding based on kindness and intuition, in written form. There may have been others but we have no record of that thinking now.

Over the course of the next 2000 years, trainers such as Dom Duarte, Federico Grisone, Giovanni Battista Pignatelli, Antoine de Pluvinel [*The Manege Royal*, Xenophon Press 2015], François Robichon de la Guérinière [*Ecole de Cavalerie*, Xenophon Press 2015], de Menezes known as Marques de Marialva practiced the art of riding, some with more, some with less, focus on humane training practices.

King Duarte (1391–1438) was called the King Philosopher. He wrote *Livro de Cavalgar* (*Book of Horsemanship*) around 1434 and dedicated it to his wife the Queen. He was ahead of his time as he applied psychology to the education of the knights in order to show them different aspects of the horses.

"It is an entirely original book. The King does not speak of what he has heard but what he has learned from great practice, the fruit of his own experience and reflection" Dom Diogo de Bragança [*Dressage in the French Tradition*, Xenophon Press 2011].

In 1575 Monsieur de Lugny stated as an explanation of the word "aids" that "the only way the horse can indicate his opinion is by resisting. By using the AIDS, we are helping him to understand what we want."

He meant that the "aids" should be an explanation of what we want, and they should "aid" the horse to understand. When aids are heavy, constant, tight, unrelenting, used as a weapon against our horse, then we create resistance rather than an explanation the horse can understand.

Every era has some true horsemen that are concerned with the reality of the communication for the well-being of the horse.

Azulejos, Detail from Alcobaca Palace, Photo by Dominique Barbier

> *"The caress itself is the very language for the horse, by which we can talk to them. The horse who is used to it would be easy to train. That is why before everything we must start with the caress in order to be able to use it in all the following lessons."*
> —Louis de Chardon sieur de Lugny 1597

Caress for partnership, Orgulho das Mangueiras with Harriet Bullit Photo by Keron Psillas

Later, Antoine Comte d'Aure, François Baucher, Gustav Steinbrecht, General L'Hotte, Etienne Beudant, Nuno Oliveira, Diogo de Bragança among others, all left important treatises, methods, and principles to guide today's participants in Classical or Academic Equitation.

Each of these Masters added their own personal touch. We need to mention François Baucher as he was instrumental in adapting the old schools to the modern Thoroughbred. His methods were ever changing as it was the era of the beginning of scientific thought which he tried to apply to his horses. That being said, he was one of the innovative geniuses.

We advise anyone truly interested in the Art of Riding to study and read these Masters' works.

Even for the horses going to war, there needed to be some sort of relationship with the horse.

Hunters, the farmer in his field, the milk deliverer, each needed a relationship with their horse and horses needed basic training to communicate and do their job. Transportation for everybody was by horse, if you were fortunate, otherwise you walked.

The beginning of the Renaissance came at a time when some of the cruelest practices, spurs and bits etc. were common. This era also gave birth to the age of enlightenment and further refinement in horsemanship, opening the door for François de la Guérinière to build upon Pignatelli (1525-1558) and Pluvinel (1552 – 1620) teachings in the mid 1700's.

Happiness, Joy. Larapio Coimbra. Photo by Keron Psillas

The F. E. I. members knew that different schools, namely French & German, would compete together and it was important that both methods would, in the end, produce similar harmonious results. The rules were put into place to level the field amongst different types of horses competing together. The English Thoroughbred, the Selle Français, the Lipizzaner, the Portuguese Lusitano could all compete together because they would be judged on proper training.

For example, extended trot was defined, so that no matter if a smaller horse with lighter gaits was showing against a bigger moving heavier horse, the judge had a prescribed criterion to use. If the extension was on the bit, light in the bridle, showing over stride and rhythm in a true trot, that was the criteria the judge could use, to avoid judgments on a preferred style of horse.

Early F. E. I. members were concerned about preserving training principles and methods so that the judges would all have a common understanding about what is correct and what should be rewarded in competition. These rules would apply worldwide, no matter if in France, Germany, United States, Brazil or anywhere else in the world.

Dressage was to preserve the happy athlete, light, round, responsive.

What is seen so very often today in competition is quite the opposite. Today we see pictures of horses with bleeding mouths and flanks, necks so grotesquely bent that they are even touching their own chest. We see horses in competition that are fearful, uncomfortable, angry, with wringing tails, frightened eyes, and miserable. Today we see horses ridden with such a heavy hand that even in the so-called extended gaits, the curb bit is pulled all the way horizontal to the ground, the contact is so heavy.

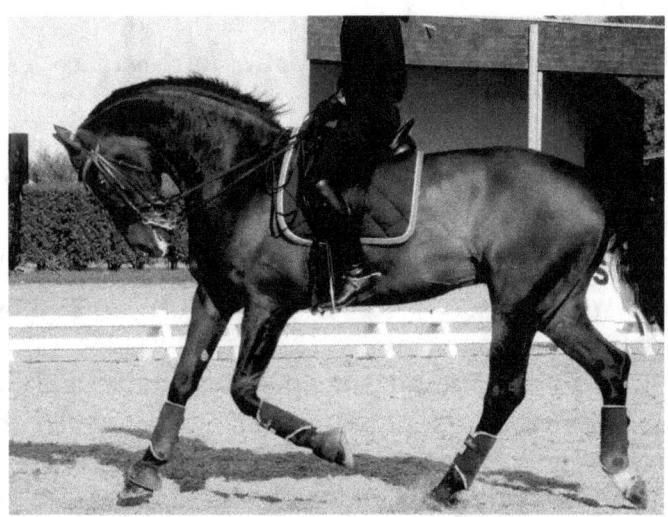

UNHAPPY HORSE Abusive Over-bending

We know of horses deprived of water to make them ridable in front of audiences. We see horses tense and ready to bolt even leaving arenas and galloping away. And these are the very horses and riders that are "winning" at competition!

We see riders pushing, forcing, spurring, whipping, and banging legs to force horses to 'perform'. We see nosebands cranked tight around horses' jaws. A new style of noseband even appeared a few years back called the CRANK, because its design enabled leverage to literally crank the horse's mouth shut, making "deglutition" relaxing of the lower jaw impossible. This has nothing whatsoever to do with what Dressage is supposed to be about. Abusive practices are becoming more and more accepted and normalized in the competitive show world.

This has even led to the addition of rules defining the code of conduct and defining financial fines for abuse, because the abuse and lack of ethics are now so common.

We have read the rules all the way back to the 1958 versions, in French and English. It struck us that the language, the verbiage, the intention is truly kind and soft. The whole tone and feeling are sensitive, positive and based on knowledge. These rules do not translate or corresponded to what we witness in competition even at the highest level today.

"We must fight, we must win against the horse" is a *direct* quote taken very recently from a five-star German judge.

Harmony, lightness, ease of movement, horse moving by himself, trusting, free, supple, with lively impulsion, graceful elasticity, neck elegantly bent are all spoken of as goals.

The back of the horse supple and vibrating, the shoulder free and light.

The horse submits himself generously to the control of the rider.

The hands *moelleux* (soft) contact, the light mouth, no resistance, grace, unobtrusiveness of riders' aids, no visible effort.

Slightest indication of the rider giving life and spirit to the body of the horse (Article 401 2003).

All of the words and phrases listed above are intentional as they portray the spirit in which we should be training. They define the relationship we are seeking.

We find all that we need in these documents. If we can heed the spirit, the gift of the intentions, listen to our predecessors, we will stay on the right path. If we choose not to honor the F. E. I. founders, we will go down the wrong path.

In the past, even the judges were encouraged to discuss together and come to an agreement on their personal appreciation of movements. At competition, judges would observe a horse and rider that were not competing that day, to discuss their different points of view.

The 1963 Prix St George was defined as a show of classical principles where lightness and suppleness must be shown.

Article 411 of the 1963 F.E.I. rules says (In French) that the Grand Prix is a test of *artistic equitation* showing perfect lightness, with absence of resistance and shows Classical High School movements.

It is interesting to note that today the definition is:

"The Grand Prix is a *competition* of the highest level, which bring out the horses perfect lightness characterized by a total absence of resistance and the complete development of collection and impulsion. The test includes all the school paces and all the fundamental airs of the Classical High School of which the *"artificial paces based on an extreme extension of the fore legs has no part."*

This makes us wonder then, why extended trots showing extreme extension of the legs is rewarded. It should receive a score of at most insufficient.

Also, please notice the versions are very different. The Grand Prix test has changed in spirit and intent. This is not a welcome or progressive change.

All throughout all versions of F. E. I. rules including today, the word *lightness* is everywhere. This is because *lightness* is an overriding fundamental aspect for Classical equitation. It is in all historical versions of the rules because it is so very important. Today *lightness* is not seen, nor recognized, not valued, not enforced, and is ignored by riders, trainers and judges alike. This is a travesty for the horses. Ignorance of *lightness* is a major reason that we are in so much trouble in Dressage today.

The very same can be said for the term *suppleness*.

In the 1963 Version, Article 411 says (In French) that the aim of lateral movements is to bring the balance and the pace (gait) into harmony. They (lateral movements) supple all parts of the horse, increasing especially the relaxation of the lower jaw process, "deglutition."

In Shoulder-In, the inside *legs pass and cross* in front of the outside legs. The bend of the horse is more or less accentuated to the degree of lateral suppleness the rider seeks to obtain.

Also, in the 1963 Rules (In French), the Shoulder-in was described as a movement to be done at 45 degrees, with crossing of the legs. In the caption it is called a two-track movement, but of course this is misnomer, as in a 45-degree angle you will see, viewed from the front or the back, 4 distinct tracks with the same spacing between the legs.

This is the four track Shoulder-In that François Robichon de la Guérinière invented.

The ultimate air of the Grand Prix test is the Piaffer. In the newest version of F. E. I. rules Piaffer is not only no longer called a trot, it is no longer required to be on the spot. The entire definition of Piaffer is changed. Quite frankly, this is because the top riders in the world can no longer do it!

The 2011 24th edition of F. E. I. states in article 415 that "Piaffer is a highly collected, cadenced, elevated diagonal movement giving the *impression* of remaining in place." We have the audacity to not even call the Piaffer a trot on the spot anymore.

In order to understand the digression of the whole system, it started with not understanding and not valuing the idea of the relaxation of the mouth and keeping the horse in a fixed head carriage for all movements.

This has led to allowing and promoting strong contact reinforced by the cranked-shut mouth and ignoring the suppleness of the hind quarters, and of the joints, and the freedom of the shoulders.

Then the digression of all lateral movements including changing the Shoulder-In from the 45-degree angle to a 30-degree angle, which allows total rigidity from beginning to end, was starting to be practiced. This change was introduced in the 1971 version of the rules. The change of angle allows the rider to retain rigidity instead of increasing suppleness, which is the very purpose and goal of sideways movements. Since then, we have seen a consistent increase in tense and rigid horses in competition.

See the drawings we have included, which are directly reproduced from the F. E. I. rule books.

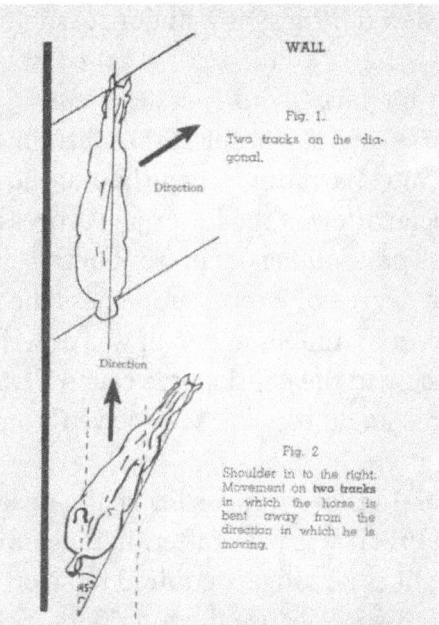

45 DEGREE SH IN: The 45-degree angle allowed the correct 4 track positioning of Shoulder-In

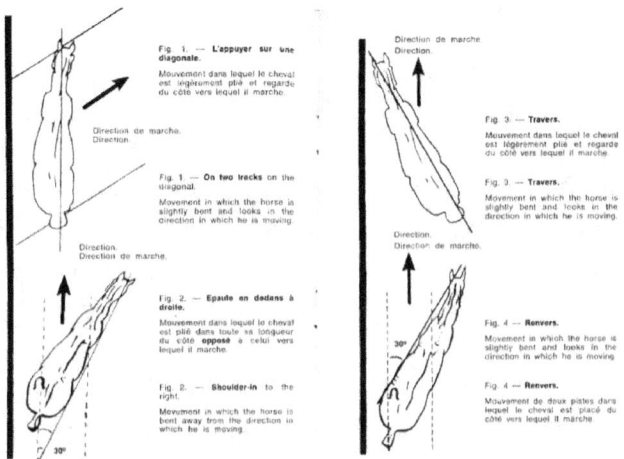

30 DEGREES: The 30-degree angle denies the purpose of the Shoulder-In by allowing the horse to maintain rigidity

> "Suppleness and relaxation are the biggest lie of the modern Dressage industry."
> —Dominique Barbier

So now that we have compromised true collection and true suppleness, we have a Grand Prix horse that is unable to perform the Piaffer. He is compressed, and rigid with a locked jaw and back. Nor can he perform a quality Passage, which is judged by the true suspension in relaxation. This is a monumental digression from Classical principles.

We have so few competitors that can obtain the Piaffer anymore, that we have had to change the rules. This is an embarrassment and an abandonment of the ultimate test of collection.

The great irony is that in the artistic dressage population, we have seen a huge increase in riders and horses able to show some Piaffer.

In the 1958 version, article 406 for Submission states "at all paces at slight flexion of the jaw, without nervousness, is a criterion of the obedience of the horse and of the harmonious distributions of his forces."

It is important to note here that this is a translation from French which is not perfectly translated into English. It is close. What is important is to understand that the horse is meant to play softly, calmly with the bit with a soft lower jaw, in deglutition. (*"Leger murmure"* in French, a light whisper in English).

"Distribution of his forces" means that he is in balance, as well as mobile, ready to move in any direction with the greatest ease at any time. This is in fact, also a definition of collection.

As we can see, language and translation can be tricky. If the translator does not wholly understand both the principles and expertly speak both languages, the meaning can be missed or misunderstood. Further if the translator has not experienced the feeling, then the essence of what is being said can be lost. We have missed the spirit of what is being portrayed.

The rules were altered in 1979 to state that the horse can show light chewing on the bit but it is no longer required.

In 1963, in Article 406 (In French) for Submission says: Submission has to show light mobility of the jaw. In other words, submission is proven by the mobility of the jaw.

This submission is for the horse, not against the horse. It is for his relaxation and ease.

The National Federation of Germany now has a segment of Baroque Equitation where you can get a certification as a Baroque instructor. Why is there such a need for this? Why are there two parallel ideas and organizations?

CHAPTER 3
THE STATE OF DRESSAGE TODAY

The state of competitive Dressage is getting progressively worse and many people feel more and more disconnected from the horses and themselves.

We have used some very strong language in this book, but it is important to talk about what is happening now. For if we do not, then we are complicit in the situation that is increasingly becoming the norm for the competitive Dressage world.

We need to be very strong in order to perhaps stop and hopefully reverse the process. We will give ample examples of what is happening today and why. We will show the progression that has led to the current disastrous situation. We need to return to putting the horse first while simultaneously preserving the art of riding.

In 2019 25th Edition for F.E.I. rules ARTICLE 419 OBJECT
OF INTERNATIONAL DRESSAGE EVENT States:
"The F. E. I. established an International Dressage Event in 1929 in order to preserve the Equestrian Art from the abuses to which it can be exposed and to preserve it in the purity of its principles, so that such principles of the discipline could be handed down intact to future generations of Athletes."

There it is in black & white. This is far from where we are today. Knowledge is being lost; misunderstanding is being spread as truth. Art is being lost. Horses are being hurt. Principles that were established to protect horses are rapidly disappearing.

Prior to 2003 the definition of Grand Prix was a competition of artistic value. Then the rules changed and now Grand Prix is defined as a competition of the highest level. There is no more mention of art. This change in mission and attitude has been very destructive, and has led to a departure from Classical principles.

We will offer some solutions to at least make your horse happier. We see restraining techniques that translate into complete over-bending as normal today.

We see the marks in tests completely inflated and not corresponding to the performances. Scores of 9 and 10 are commonly given.

The rules of the F. E. I. are not being respected, (even by that very body itself), judges are not asked to uphold the rules and we are not respecting our horses.

Competition today most often shows an artificial mechanized trot which has nothing to do with Dressage.

While we don't wish to blame any individuals nor the F. E. I., it is necessary to expose some of the practices and the intentions. We speak of, and to, the F. E. I. a great deal in the following pages, but it is not meant to place blame. Blame is not meant to be placed with any individual, but the organization must be held accountable to maintain its very own mission.

The F. E. I. legacy is to preserve the Equestrian Art and its Classical principles. We cannot afford to squander this legacy, for it is of critical importance to the future of horses and riders, as the founders knew.

From its inception the F. E. I. mission was to protect horses by means of Classical principles. They need our support, now more than ever, to be courageous in upholding this mission. There is no other body that can carry this torch. The pressures are very great, we realize, for political, financial and populist reasons. They have taken some admirable steps but they need to oblige the judges to respect the rules, or admit it is time to openly change the rules.

> *"We must apply the rules or change them. I am not for the change of the rules but for the respect of them, as they defend and protect the horses."*
> —Dominique Barbier

TODAY
WHAT HAS GONE WRONG

We are going in the wrong direction in the competitive world due to issues of judging, attitude, training, and ethics.

The consequences of the slow and steady deconstruction of the previous rules and the blatant non respect of the current rules is leading to a destruction of the very essence of Dressage.

Horses have been, and are being, exploited and abused over and over again, with the complicity for the F. E. I., the judges, and the competitors. They are exploited for greed and power. This situation is unbelievably cruel. In fact, it is cruel to horses *and* riders that truly wish to compete with honest intentions.

We believe that the pressure to perform, to win every time and all the time is taking a gigantic toll, even on the top riders in the competitive world today.

The pressure to perform is driven by the money that is fueling the horse industry. Today we can say "stop the abuse." Money and the lack of education of riders and judges has led to the mistreatment of the horse, even if only by ignorance rather than intent.

The situation is tragic. The basic welfare of the horses is not respected and how can we judge an event without respecting the rules?

There is a total misconception of the values that the original F. E. I. mission was meant to safeguard.

One of the deconstructions of the rules is meant to favor horses with huge gaits and puts the emphasis on big movement versus the higher training in collection.

For example, judging of big natural gaits ridden in rigidity are very different than judging trained collected Passage/Piaffer transitions. The advantage is being given to horses with big gaits, not collection, and does not show the ability of the rider/trainer nor the horse.

Precision is now rewarded and valued more than relaxation and beauty. Dressage tests are designed for showing many flying changes, which are much easier to show on a rigid horse, than a truly collected pirouette in a three-beat canter on a relaxed horse.

Dressage is not a *"modele et allure"* show or breed contest. The reward is being given to these big gaits, and not to properly collected and trained horses.

> *"The coefficient should be proportional to the difficulty of the movement."*
> —Dom Diogo de Bragança, from his book
> *Dressage in the French Tradition* [Xenophon Press 2011]

Because the wrong assumption that bigger gaits are more valuable than more usual gaits, more and more dressage competition is rewarding breeds and breeding of horses that are bigger and have more spectacular-looking gaits. This is due to trying to gain and impress audiences that know nothing of Classical riding. Dressage is becoming a freak show. The huge giant movers showing exaggerated gaits are meant, in part, to attract audiences. In addition, when these horses are not even trained properly, we are demonstrating anti-classical principles.

The result does not allow the horse to properly use his hindquarters. It has been stated recently that we can have "positive" tension. Some justify that you can produce movements this way, in resistance. There is no such thing as *positive* tension.

Let's be clear, Tension is Tension, produced by compression.

COMPETE TO TRAIN OR TRAIN TO COMPETE

Now the norm is that you compete to train. It is expected that you must climb a level or two per show season, or you are failing. This has led amateurs and professionals alike to increase demands and put too much pressure on horses and their riders. This is leading to depression in horses, riders and trainers.

Some trainers are even beginning to speak up, in the press, about the pressure to perform and win all the time. This is so unreasonable.

Dressage tests are supposed to be judged on each horse and rider *on that day, in that test*. Now, the expectation is that one of three or four riders (that won the most recent competition) will be placed first, no matter what the performance. The placing of many events is now nearly automatic and a foregone conclusion. This encourages the expectation of perfection on demand. No horse or rider can live up to that every single day. Only three riders out of classes of 20 or more horses can win. So, we have set up our competitors and owners to feel that they failed if the test of the day was not the winning one. This leads to undue pressure and abuse of horses and even riders!

EXPECTATIONS

We have set up an expectation that the judges must also place the same horses and riders on top, or they risk ridicule. It is a popularity contest now. And often, sadly, is a contest of whose horse is the biggest! This is not fair to anyone involved. Even audiences are beginning to question and voice their concern that what they are witnessing is correct. People who are artistic recognize there is no art or heart in the performance.

Dressage & CT magazine in the March 1977 edition included an interview with Dominique. He was asked at that time what he thought about the competitive world.

"I want the competition to serve the horse, that the horse would be better afterwards." "Now I would like to see people compete with their horses, not against their horses."

We have included the entire article as an appendix to this book.

New tests designed by incompetent or inexperienced committee members put in unexplainable changes every other year with no logical progression.

For more than 40 years we have seen situations in the US of riders with one successful horse under their belt, being put in the position of being trainers at a national level. Indeed, trainers of trainers are often inexperienced, and may have only trained one or two horses.

Judging education programs often face the same problem.

As a trainer should know, we start with the beginning of collection before lengthening. This is a very classical principle. That way the horse never gets hurt. If we wish to change the tests, they still need to be based on the principles of training, and not change the spirit nor the foundation of the Classical training practices.

CHANGE OF PHILOSOPHY OF TRAINING

When the F. E. I. was established, there weren't professional 'trainers,' it was the military people and a few select individuals riding and training. So, the meetings and competitions were something that was friendly and with an idea of sharing practices and ideas. As recently as the 1970s the horse show community was friendly. They were a group of riders that wanted to share ideas and enjoy their horses. They would even invite fellow competitors to ride each other's horses.

The difference back then was money had not infiltrated the culture. Now the competitor that is winning, the breeder that is winning, stands to make fortunes. The introduction of very big money has polluted the show world. This is not in the Dressage world alone, of course. The tragedy is that Dressage is supposed to represent the ultimate in educated riding. If the upper echelon of riding and training cannot be sustained in a pure form, then the entire horse world is in jeopardy.

It has become a multi-billion-dollar industry on the International level, and with no thought to friendliness and relationship with your horse or with other competitors.

It used to be that we would train and then compete two levels below what we were working on at home. You would never "show" work that you were working on at home. We would never show in a level that was not easy and confirmed for the horse, which allowed for relaxation and joy at the show. The show ring was not a place to train.

Economically, the horse industry is getting bigger and bigger. Bigger prize money is producing more and more expensive horses. This encourages business people to go into the horse industry and horses are treated as a commodity.

> *"The Germans blame the Dutch; the Dutch blame the Germans.*
> *The French blame everybody."*
> —Dominique Barbier

Some judges are prone to placing their own nations above others. Judges are often spread far apart as far as scores given. This means that the judge's education has no continuity and is not based on the same criteria.

The goal of Classical schools is to value beauty and spirit that can be shared with your horse. Classical art form is different in goals and nature than competition.

Dressage Competition is now based on a "pyramid of training."

The feeling for the horse, the beauty is no longer factored. Now we train our horse only to perform tests.

COLLECTION VERSUS COMPRESSION

In the Classical art of riding, collection leads to lightness. These days compression leads to more and more contact, with a loss of lightness. The contact results in use of force and resistance for training. We are now training in rigidity. Dressage is supposed to be harmony in suppleness not compression in rigidity.

Compression in rigidity creates many of the problems in Piaffer, Passage, and keeping the correct canter in Pirouette.

The rule for Piaffer used to be, that it was to be performed on the spot. Now, because no one can show a proper Piaffer, instead of teaching trainers, riders, and judges to correctly train and evaluate the movement, they have simply changed the rule to say that a Piaffer is no longer required to be on the spot.

They're unable to Piaffe correctly because the horses are compressed instead of properly collected, and not in the proper balance, in order to give the movement. When they ask for Piaffer if they can't push the horse forward, they simply stall out, they are so stuck, again because of the misunderstanding that horses need to be pushed to Piaffe.

If you have collected your horse properly and he is light in hand and mentally forward the Piaffer is no problem. The belief that the horse needs to be pushed to go forward versus the belief that the horse will walk, trot and canter, Passage and Piaffer on his own with the rider who is present and leading the dance is a cultural difference.

DOMINIQUE BARBIER AND LIZ CONROD

Piaffer in Descente de Main, Descente de Jambes, in Lightness. This is always possible without force of any kind. Sedoso ridden by Dominique Barbier Photo by Candida von Braun

Compressing the horse makes him uncomfortable and can lead to real pain. The unhappy horse can have a physical and mental breakdown that makes him fearful of everything. We have seen a world champion Dressage horse totally out of control and panicked in Germany during the award ceremony a few years ago. The slave-master relationship, uses intimidation, force and punishment with fear energy to train. Nervous energy creates mental rigidity.

HOLDING & FORCED CONTACT

In the modern Dressage, since we have stopped looking for lightness, which means self-carriage with only the weight of the leather as contact, we have accepted holding contact. Holding has become the norm, and even desirable. This holding contact has created a lot of discomfort especially when the horse is held in the wrong position, which is most often the case.

Horses are perpetually, constantly over-bent and behind the vertical.

Forced into grossly over-bent position, so wrong,
but this picture is so common it is assumed to be correct now.

Forcing contact by constant movement of hand and, or the half-halt, forcing forward movement by constant squeezing, kicking and spurring with back pushing and driving seat is the start of the destruction of the balance we are seeking. Confused riders constantly disturb the horse. Resistance is provoked in our horse. Yet we blame the horse for the very resistance we have created.

Forcing and holding contact is now a vicious cycle. Now we arrive at the horse over-bent and disconnected.

Suppleness and relaxation are the biggest lies in the horse industry. People are now using rigidity and resistance for training instead.

Rollkur was first witnessed in the warmup competition ring, when it was demonstrated by what are supposed to be the best and most educated riders in the world.

Thus, we became aware that this was now a commonly used training technique. This is a system of over-bending the horse to such an extreme that even people that know nothing at all about horses were appalled. In addition to severe over-bending, the extreme tightness of the cranked noseband produces an excessive salivation by preventing the horse to deglutinate. Not only is the neck in a paralyzing position but the jaw, mouth and head of the horse are locked and tortured. This sent us down a path of extreme abuse of horses.

Because these riders were *winning*, so many began to believe that it was a good, correct method. We will pay the price for this egregious idea for years to come.

"We must fight, we must win against the horse."
again, is a *direct* quote taken very recently from a five-star German judge.

This practice has perpetrated as much pain on horses as the hideous practice of soring gaited horses.

This particular abuse of forcing a horse's nose down to its chest, with its neck bent half way down the vertebrae is practiced by even top International riders. This painful, grotesque practice is touted as a way to get the horse to be supple and obedient.

In fact, what this method really does, is to totally disconnect the horses back and make it completely numb, both physically and mentally.

There was finally enough outcry, even by uneducated audiences, that the F. E. I. decreed Rollkur as unacceptable in 2010.

Now we call it L. D. R. and it is still sanctioned by the F. E. I., as they claim it does not use undue force.

The F. E. I. totally let horses down by not defining L. D. R. as an outrageous practice. This has led to thousands of riders believing this is correct, all the way down to back yard dressage enthusiasts. It is now so pervasive it will take a generation to cleanse this picture of how a Dressage horse (and others) should look. It is a painful, destructive practice, totally contrary to Dressage principles, and ethics and permanently damages horses' minds and backs.

Very common picture today, and at first glance looks OK. However, the horse is over-bent, not drastically, but enough to have compromised the connection and his back.

This culture has led to the universal idea that over-bent horses, and being behind the vertical is acceptable at all levels. Any knowledgeable rider or trainer knows that as soon as the horse is over-bent he disappears. His mind is now incapable of being engaged. This syndrome is similar to the reaction of abused people. And it HURTS. It is so accepted that even horses being ridden on the long rein are now seen behind the vertical.

The consequences of the change of rules and the acceptance of over-bending horses has deteriorated the *very essence* of Dressage which is the *purity of the gaits*.

Educate the judges, or change the rules for Sport Horses, but do not call it Dressage. Let's apply the rules to protect the horses.

You cannot open a magazine, watch a Dressage video, go to a Dressage show from the local small town all the way to the top International level and not find most horses in an over-bent position. We must educate judges and trainers.

Recently I heard a local instructor laugh, as he explained, to a student that "she better not ride in her show as she was training, (the horse was behind the vertical) as she might get demerits."

I thought to myself "I can only pray she'd get demerits for over bending her horse!" Liz.

Brutality is evidenced by blood on horses' mouths and sides, blue tongues are caused by over-tight nose bands. The deluxe sponsors of International competition have blood on their hands. In addition to Rollkur, draw reins, bamboo poles for beating legs, incorrect curb adjustment, are used by ignorant trainers to obtain quick results.

Even more violent, we now employ crank nosebands, leading to blue tongues as they exert so much force that the horse cannot even swallow. We are supposed to be promoting the relaxation of the lower jaw, but now the idea is to lock the horses jaw, face and head so tight they cannot even breathe properly, let alone swallow. This is NOT Dressage! Such cruelty.

Remember, the relaxation of the lower jaw produces the deglutition, which is the essence of the soft harmonious mouth that leads to lightness.

Then, if the abusive training techniques do not produce the expected results we turn to drugs. If drugs don't work, or turn out to be detectable, next, they take away the horses' water for a number of days to make him controllable. If that does not work then they bleed them to deny them the very source of life itself. All these practices are intended to weaken the horse, as he is considered our enemy, and are simply a means to an end for our personal gain. Horses die at competitions from dehydration now. This is a world scandal.

> *"We must fight, we must win against the horse"*
> is a *direct* quote taken very recently from a five-star German judge.

This sad quote is repeated here, not to promote it but because this seems to be such a pervasive idea. So many riders do not even realize that the way they approach training is to subjugate and enslave the horse. When you think in terms of push, drive, make, more (of everything), when your trainer uses these words the feeling is that your horse is an instrument, a vehicle. This is not happiness. This does not lead to the happy athlete.

This attitude is despicable. This thinking is outrageous but a very popular and shared idea. What a tragedy.

In Europe there are horse mills, similar to our puppy mills, where horses are being trained but then destroyed if they are not up to the standard and able to endure one specific training method applied to all of them.

People are under Non-Disclosure Contracts to keep the silence. If the horse is not likely to be the one individual to be worth millions, he is completely expendable. In Europe, nearly sixty percent of insured horses are dead before they are eight years old.

The problem with this approach to training is that they have only one way of doing things. If the horse does not fit into their singular method, they determine that the horse cannot be trained. The classical training is the reverse, where we must adapt our approach to the need of each individual.

Young horses are routinely injected in the hocks in an effort to preserve the soundness, as so many break down due to the training imposed on them. This is a very common practice on the Quarter Horses. The F. E. I. has taken a stand against this, and needs to do a better job with Dressage horses as well.

Riding in force against the horse, cranked closed mouths, training techniques such as Rollkur have no place in the relationship with your partner. Your partner, your horse, is not your enemy.

Horses have been abused by many disciplines and for many reasons over the centuries. What is most shameful is that Dressage is supposed to be the epitome of cultured and educated riding and training, yet the Dressage community turns a blind eye. This is due in part to the huge financial investment in the horse industry.

Please, understand that we know, that *not all* participants behave this way. But the silence makes us all complicit. The best trainers, the best riders, the best owners must speak up and speak out. Rather than follow the trend of "winners," when the wrong path is taken, our community should stay true to principles that have guided us from the beginning of the F. E. I. laying down the rules in the first place. This can take great courage, but if we do not stand up for the horses, they have no protector.

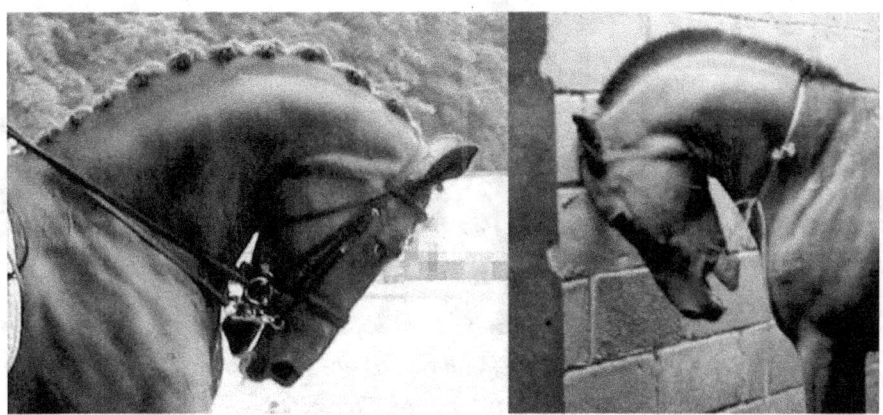

TORTURE. Horses are being tortured every day in the name of supposedly "Modern Dressage."

WHAT DO WE WANT DRESSAGE COMPETITION TO BE?

*Happy Light Horse, this is what Dressage is meant to be. Escoteiro ridden by Sarah Scheerer.
Photo by Rebekah McNeff*

Beauty in Shoulder-In, round, light, happy, . Galan ridden by Caylee Sparry Photo by Diane Williams

    Do we want Dressage competition to be based on a classical basis of all schools together or would we like Dressage to be more physical and sportive and therefore less harmonious? We must act in the spirit of F. E. I. Article 401, for the Happy Horse and Article 419 for International Competition.

    If we choose sport then article 419 will be rendered obsolete. Article 401 again, states, "The object of Dressage is the development of the Horse into a Happy Athlete through *harmonious* education."

    If we choose competition as it stands today, over Art and Harmony we must have the honesty and the courage to delete or change articles 401, and 419. Otherwise we will discredit the F. E. I. itself. This would be sad indeed.

Perfect four track Shoulder-In. Direction, Rhythm, Bend, Lightness. , Herodes DB ridden by Sarah Richter. Photo by Davi Carrano

We see riders in competition so often taking an offensive position. The hands are too forward, too high, without feeling, driving the horse forward with an armchair seat in an orthopedic saddle. They are bracing against the horse, with constant kicking or squeezing legs and spur trying to force, and hold the horse into a compressed position. It is not surprising then, when horses rebel, disconnect and hurt themselves. Then they believe the solution is more leg, more half-halts, more force, more compressing. . . it is a sad situation, worse and worse.

> *"They do not change method, they change horses."*
> —Dominique Barbier

They tell themselves this one is not good, not very suitable for Dressage. Bring another! How many failures do you need before questioning the method and even yourself?

Why do we see so many compressed, rigid horses so often in competition now? Why does the trot no longer even look like a trot? Why are spectators wondering if so called "Dressage" is supposed to look like this?

There are several reasons. First, the sad truth is that the horse world (as well as so many other worlds these days) is run by money and lots of it. It is very expensive to campaign horses on the International and even the national level today. Horses are more expensive, access to trainers that can teach riders what to exhibit to win are expensive.

Most riders do not even own the horses they are competing with today. Corporations do.

Money rules the day in the horse world now, as it does in so many areas. The extra tragedy is that horses are paying the price. Winning competitors can now expect huge endorsement opportunities, can command huge training fees from owners that want to win. Often these owners are not even individuals but conglomerates whose goal is return on financial investment. Judges are either unwilling to go against the tide or lack the knowledge to understand that what they are rewarding is incorrect. It is politically and financially unwise to place an International competitor below the rank that she (or he) gained in the last competition. Judges that do know better are leaving the profession in defeat and disgust.

In November 2018, The F. E. I. terminated its relationship with National Reining Horse Association and the American Quarter Horse Association. The reasons given were continued use of banned substances (drugs), allowing horses too young to compete and stewarding violations. I applaud the F. E. I. for taking a stand, enforcing its own rules.

This step is to be commended, but the Dressage competitive world is also in need of much more stringent upholding of the rules.

Young horse on the way to Descente de Main, Descente de Jambes. , Herodes DB ridden by Lauren Schultz. Photo by Kelsey Welter

AQHA and NRHA felt that the main responsibility for the welfare of the horse rests with the rider, but riders and trainers were abusing the rules. It is the F. E. I.'s job to uphold its very own rules to protect the happy athlete. Even a child can look at a horse being ridden in L. D. R. position and know the horse is uncomfortable. This is not the horses' choice! Where is progression through understanding here? Where is the comfort? Only when the rider gets *off!*

Due to this picture being presented constantly to young riders and trainers, the perpetually behind the bit horse now looks normal and correct. Everywhere we look these days, from our very own back yard to pictures of International competition the exception is to see a horse *not* over-bent, *not* behind the bit. And we are so deeply saddened because the very nature of Dressage training is meant to teach the horse to comfortably carry the rider. *These horses are neither comfortable nor happy.*

In 2019, a major article about Dressage in a US national horse magazine was about how to attract audiences to make Dressage competition financially viable. It is absolutely true that horse sport competitions are expensive. Winning horses and horses displaying traits that are popular in the show ring command huge prices. Today, if a young horse is 16 hands or larger and shows huge gaits it is very easy to sell, even better, if the horse shows huge movement in big gaits. Breeders fortunes are based on prizes and medals earned worldwide, add to this how fashion plays into what is popular and promoted. The very reason the F. E. I. was founded was to guard against the very results we are seeing today.

In America, for the last several decades, one would not have dreamed of taking a horse under age five into competition. And they started at training level.

They would rarely progress more than one or one and a half levels per year. Why? Because it was known that it took about a year or even more to go up the levels. Because it takes time to train a horse mentally and physically. A Grand Prix horse took 7 or 8 years to develop. So, they were at *least* ten years old and more often, twelve years old or above. Of course, you can have a very gifted horse that progresses faster but that is an exception. If you do not take the time you end up compromising and most often the horse pays the price. Now the trend is to compete before the horse is ready to easily participate in the tests it is given. Training for competition is its own method, built around tests. Collection is gained by more force. The progression and time that a horse needs is given little value. If you are competing and you show up in the show ring at the same level for more than a year you are thought to be failing. Suspension created by rigidity is imposed on the horse to impress judges that no longer have the education to know the difference. Or if they do, there is so much pressure to reward what is popular that they dare not judge correctly lest they don't get hired next time.

There is nothing wrong with training big horses with very big gaits for competition. The problem is that we are compromising the horses' well-being in the pursuit of trophies and building audiences.

Totilas before and after. The picture speaks for itself.

The rewards of winning are great in today's world. The trainer/riders stand to make lots of money if they are winning, not to mention establishing a lucrative teaching, training and often breeding business as well. Conversely if you do not have major financial resources you are not going to National and certainly not International competitions without a well-heeled sponsor, who wants to see a return on their investments. So, the pressure to perform and win is very great.

Now we are seeing the attitude of: "if you need to deny your very big and strong horse some water at the competition, so be it. If you need to go hide behind the barn to obtain your Piaffer, so be it. If the owner of the horse you are paid to ride wants you to push forward when the horse is not ready, so be it."

Make no mistake, all of this is happening in the competition world. Time is money. This theory leads to the belief that if you take shortcuts you are better off. In fact, correct training does not take much more time, just more knowledge. The result is very different for the horse and rider when time and understanding have been allowed. We are looking for the beauty in the harmonious relationship and that cannot be done by shortcuts and forcing.

Now we see horses in competition that have worried eyes, wringing tails, tense jaws, tight backs. Yet, if the horse can do 25 changes in the test, can fling his front legs forward (while not even tracking up!) when asked for an extended trot then they often win anyway. Especially if they are very *big*.

> *"This came home to me in a very sad way. I have a friend with a nice mare that I have been helping for few years now. I am a Dressage teacher. I teach everyone, no matter if they want to ride trails, jump, event or anything else, to put their horse on the bit, and round, to ride with the light and soft leg and hand.*
>
> *My friend stopped abruptly in the middle of our lesson a while back and said to me "You know, I don't really want to ride Dressage" I was stunned and asked her why. She replied "Dressage riders are all so stiff, tight and look unhappy. I am looking for a connection with my horse and that is not what dressage looks like to me" I asked her why she thought this. "When I see competitions on TV, I don't see any connection between horse and rider. Horses and riders are not happy, but stiff and rigid."*
>
> *And she is right. We discussed further that what is so often seen in top competition is not classical Dressage, but what is in fashion now, what is promoted as being of higher interest to audiences. I suspect that there are many many people that feel the same way my friend does and they are ready to write Dressage off."*
>
> —Liz

What is on display in the Dressage Competition world will have two effects. One is that, as the story above demonstrates, many will be turned off Dressage and this is a very sad state of affairs. The other effect, perhaps much more destructive is that young people (and older ones too—the fastest growing Dressage enthusiast population is women 50 and over) will start to believe that what they see winning ribbons is correct and legitimate Dressage. If an art form is not practiced and learned it can be lost. Very few competitive riders today, have ever read books or the teachings from history. We suspect that not one competitor under 40 has read a single book by Nuno Oliveira, or de La Guérinière... All of the teaching and education of competitive riders comes from other competitors, and most often those that have won major titles.

The danger is that the principles practiced and being rewarded in show rings are heading down the very wrong path. True collection has been compromised and is now more often compression. True lightness is not only not taught, but even condemned in the show ring.

If you have a small loop in the rein you are said to have lost "contact." Michel Henriquet tells us that his wife, Catherine Durand had to fake it and show contact when showing, even though lightness was practiced at home. How are classical principles ever to survive in a world where tense, rigid unhappy horses ridden with a heavy hand and leg are held up as ideals?

The F. E. I. has the final word over what is to be allowed and valued in the show ring. For this reason, that is the body that we must look to, to help solve the problems we see now. But the F. E. I. must also be made aware that it matters to the Dressage community, and we must support them in implementing the enforcement and education that is needed.

The beauty of the ART is very rarely seen in today's competitions. Artistic concerns are being overshadowed by business concerns. How do we get audiences to come, how do we pay ourselves for the time it takes to train a horse? How do we compete on a level field if our horses are not very big, with very big and pronounced trots? How do I get hired as a judge if I don't place the same rider that won the last time in first place? How can I afford the time it takes to really learn to ride, train or judge? These are questions that many in the business of Dressage are asking. There is no problem without a solution. Education may be able to reverse the trends.

United Nations Educational, Scientific and Cultural Organization (UNESCO) established its *Lists of Intangible Cultural Heritage* with the aim of ensuring better protection of important intangible cultural heritages.

In 2011 UNESCO added French Riding tradition to this important list with the following statement:

"French-style horseback riding guided by principles of non-violence was one of seven items added Sunday to UNESCO's list of "intangible cultural heritage" in need of preservation."

Equitation in the French tradition emphasizes "harmonious relations between humans and horses," UNESCO explained about the latest selection on its website.

BROKEN OR BEAUTIFUL

"The common denominator among riders is the desire to establish close relations with the horse, build mutual respect and work towards achieving 'lightness.'"

Garrocha exhibition in Lightness. Quebec Alegria dos Pinhais Ridden by Jill McCrae.
Photo by Jeff Orrell

The fundamental horse-training principles and processes are guided by non-violence and lack of constraint, blending human demands with respect for the horse's body and mood. Knowledge of the animal itself (physiology, psychology, anatomy) and human nature (emotions and the body), are complemented by a horseman's state of mind that combines skill and respect for the horse. Fluidity of movements and flexibility of joints ensure that the horse participates in the exercises without coercion. Although practiced throughout France and elsewhere, the most widely known community is the Cadre Noir of Saumur, based at the National School of Equitation. The common denominator among riders is the desire to establish close relations with the horse, build mutual respect and work towards achieving 'lightness.' Cooperation between generations is strong, with respect for the experience of older riders, galvanized by the enthusiasm of younger riders.

Frequent public displays and galas hosted by the Cadre Noir of Saumur help to sustain the visibility of equitation in the French tradition.

It is worth noting here that the term Non-Violent was applied to French methods. The implication and understanding are that other methods are employing violence.

Thanks to this registration, we rediscover all the richness of French Classical Dressage, which will be available for the younger generation.

CHAPTER 4
THE EVILS OF CONTACT

"Contact is the evil destroyer of the connection between horse and rider."
—Dominique Barbier

The "contact" we are discussing here is defined as strong contact, anything more than the weight of the leather of the rein.

The only contact we want is the weight of the leather, as we are looking for the horse to be in self-carriage.

For a lot of people this strong contact is to appease their fears. They also believe they have control when they have heavy contact; it is like a security blanket.

The idea of what we call *contact* today is one of the most misunderstood concepts, and the perception of what it is and why it is needed is one of the most destructive concepts in the Dressage world today.

Traditionally, when we are participating in the mindset of *physical* riding, contact with the hands is considered the "aid" of communication with the horse. The constant contact of the leg is accepted as the only way to obtain forward motion in the horse. The contact of the seat is considered the physical aid to drive the horse forward.

The famous half-halt is the combination of action of the hands, legs and seat that is supposedly "rebalancing" the horse. Riders believe that they can physically accomplish this and further believe that they need to do so. The practice of half-halt is so excessive that some riders are using it every stride.

When we believe that all these "aids" are necessary to communicate with our horse we end up riding "mechanically."

The concept of driving aids and strong, even contact with hands with constant pushing leg and driving seat leads to unhappy mechanical horses. This produces a lot of resistance from the horse who is not comfortable physically and mentally.

There are a lot of ways to ride and train a horse. Many books have been published advising and teaching this method. Some people believe that the horse needs to be pushed and driven to go forward, others believe the horse is going forward on his own in walk, trot, canter, Passage, Piaffe, with the rider enjoying the ride. This is a cultural difference.

The concept of forcing the horse forward is not helping a harmonious relationship. Forcing horses to be happy, forcing the horse to go forward, forcing the horse to dance does not lead to beauty or art form.

WRONG UNDERSTANDING:

This forced extension with heavy contact has created an artificial trot, and the horse is now rigid and tense.

Thinking you cannot have collection without contact is a wrong understanding. Contact produces compression, rigidity, contraction, and un-levelness and later, lameness, being rein-lameness or lameness on a weak leg.

Any forcing is abusive, and causes physical and mental problems.

Contact, more than the weight of the rein, kills the possibility of relaxation that leads to self-carriage and lightness.

Extension in Lightness, Forward, Balanced, Round. Majestic. Fury, PRE Gelding ridden by Sandro Huerzeler. Photo by Martin Bruegger

Contact is the destroyer of the connection between horse and rider. Why? Because, not only do you have contact with the hand, but you have contact with leg and the seat.

This physical contact, most of the time, abused by force, is destroying the relationship that we have with the horse because physically we try to interfere with his balance. This is where the half-halt is born. . . .

Every action of the rider must start with a strong message, meaning a strong visualization, a clear picture of what we are asking. Physical action without the proper thinking of what we are asking is confusing and abusive.

If we have too much hand, then we are obliged to start using too much leg and seat. All those points of contact, used with force, are destroying the balance and our relationship with the horse because we are forcing him to do something physically. In dancing, there is no force.

Why does the training pyramid refer to contact? Because it is built on the misconception that the horse needs *us* to balance *him*. If the horse is put in the correct position for his balance, gently and softly on the bit, with enough energy to carry himself, we will not have problems of balance.

On the contrary, if we force with the hand, kick and squeeze with the leg and drive with the seat then we have a series of problems that we created by our searching for "contact," and trying to make the balance happen.

To begin with, if we pull on the mouth, the horse pulls back and the action of pulling back is going to destroy the balance, as well as create resistance and muscles in the wrong place through his tenseness. If we kick with the leg, we contract our body and the horse. . . and the first thing he will try is to escape by going too fast, and then we come back and pull (too much) with the hand. Driving with the seat is the same. Then, in competition, all the principles are based on the fact that we use contraction to train instead of searching for the relaxed, supple, happy horse.

Rigidity is created by the wrong position, and strong contact with hands and legs and seat.

Xenophon wrote:

> "For what the horse does under compulsion (as Simon also observes) is done without understanding: and there is no beauty in it either, any more than if one should whip and spur a dancer."

Draw reins, (German reins) are used to force them to be in the 'good position' but in reality, this disconnects and hurts the back of the horse, often for life. We cannot force the horse to be correct and happy.

The concept of driving aids and strong, even contact with hands with constant pushing leg and driving seat leads to unhappy mechanical horses. It produces a lot of resistance from the horse who is not comfortable physically nor mentally. The concept of forcing the horse forward does not promote a harmonious relationship. Forcing the horse to go forward, forcing the horse to dance does not lead to beauty or artistic riding. It appears as if it works, but the horse never finds happiness or comfort in a forced position. When the horse is ridden in this manner, the back is disconnected and then becomes weak. The result is not having the possibility to go through correctly and now the horse is very uncomfortable and unfit for Dressage, and can eventually become unfit to ride! This disconnection prevents the correct engagement of the hindquarters, no true collection, only forced compression.

IN DANCING, THERE IS NO FORCE. SO HOW DO WE REMEDY THIS?

In the modern Classical riding, we understand what energy is. In my book, *Dressage of the New Age,* 30 years ago, the concept of visualization was introduced to the art of riding. Of course, it always existed, reserved for a very few riders, who knew about it. The technique of visualization was made mainstream for many other sports such as tennis and golf. The development of a mental video was used to prepare the athlete for his performance. In riding, you can prepare yourself without your horse in precisely planning your sessions. It does not mean they cannot be changed; it means that you need a plan. For example, you can imagine a mental communication, a mental conversation.

The contact does not mean only physical contact, but means mental communication. In French Classical riding the ideal contact with the hand is the weight of the leather in the rein, nothing more.

This is because it will lead ultimately to *Descente de Main, Descente de Jambes,* which is the goal of Classical French Dressage.

The concept of contact with the leg is simply defined as the hand of a good dancer. The leg is *there*, but is not pushing, the leg must *breathe* with the horse. The horse will understand *"le souffle de la botte"* translated as the "whisper of the boot." The seat is the centaur's connection to the horse. Your back and his back are one, helping each other in the dance.

We never mention the half-halt, because of its complete destructive misunderstanding and execution today.

Why is half-halt so popular? Because we tell the horse to be lighter in the hand, when we created the heaviness in the first place!

The half-halt was invented because riders believe that the horses balance is "wrong." We now believe that *we* must "correct" the horse's balance, when it is us that destroyed the balance.

The correct understanding of the half-halt should be a combination of the upper part of the body, going back and upwards with the connection of the elbows to the hand allowing an invitation for the horse to sit on the haunches and therefore allowing the front to come up naturally. Of course, we do this with the intention of asking the horse to go lower behind and higher in front, to sit. We do not ask him do sit more than he is capable of at his level of training and understanding. As we will explain later, correct lunging, work in hand, Shoulder-In and Haunches-In will allow that process, with the correct mental understanding.

The half-halt was never meant to be a kick in the teeth accompanied by a kick in the belly.

A different belief is necessary for the execution. The mental half-halt is completely dependent on the fact that we believe that the horse will stay in the position without action, which he will do because he is comfortable, and understands. If we are sitting in the correct balance for the horse, we do not need to rebalance the horse in the first place. When we lean back and tall, we are asking the horse for collection, which is the sitting position in lightness.

Lightness in Energy. Xodo ridden by Debra Barbier. Photo by Keron Psillas

Article 401 says that a Happy Athlete will display "harmony, lightness and ease of the movements."

Contact has come to be understood as weight in the rider's hands and pressure of the bit against the mouth. True and real lightness is the absence of contact, and in balance. Lightness is self-carriage. This is not to say that the horse is not connected. Connection and contact have become interchangeable both in verbiage and in concept. Connection means that the horse's hind, through the back, is connected to the front. Contact is now confused with connection and this is a great misunderstanding.

Lightness is for the horse's ease and happiness as well as for the rider's ease. Correct Dressage teaches the horse to be more responsive, more in tune with his rider. A light horse can feel the smallest closing of the fingers, the slightest change in height of the hand. The horse ridden in contact has had to stiffen and tighten his jaw in order to protect himself from pressure on his sensitive mouth. Because the jaw is connected to his back and shoulders, he has blocked those as well, to protect himself and any finesse becomes impossible.

These are not new principles. Lightness has been understood for centuries, although by very few. The fad now is for larger, heavier horses being bred and used for competition in the last few decades. It has come to be accepted that these bigger moving horses cannot be light, which is simply not true. However, when we believe and decide our horses cannot be light, we make it so. It is we that made the horse heavy, not the horse!

Communication. Perfect balance, leading to lightness. Orador do Top ridden by Dominique Barbier. Photo by Melinda d'Amico

When you insist that the horse take "contact" more than the weight of the rein itself, then, in fact, you are stopping the horse. We imagine that the horse feels that he is being ridden through a closed door. He will be very uncomfortable, mentally and physically, as the force is now exerted on his mouth, and indeed all along his spine. The horse is now not very willing to go forward as he is constantly being asked to stop via pressure on the reins, and feels discomfort in his mouth, neck and back. The rider is obliged and coached to push with the leg and seat to push past the very contact that we imposed on him. The horse is no longer a dance partner. The horse will make himself as rigid as he can to protect himself! And very likely, he will be frightened, confused, angry and uncomfortable, and possibly leading to lameness.

We hear the expression all the time that the horse should "seek the contact." *NO* and *YES*.

The horse is seeking communication via lightness that would lead to balance.

Horses mimic the contact the rider gives him. If you pull, they pull. If you give, they give. Horses do not desire to lean on the steel in their mouth. They seek to feel balanced, centered, connected to the mind of the rider so that they can move comfortably.

In physical riding the amount of contact with the rein for a young horse is associated with his willingness to go forward, which is obsolete and incorrect thinking, but sadly it is frequently believed to be the truth. The young horse does not need contact to go forward.

Any horse can be forward, and *is* forward with the lightest and softest of contact.

Contact, (i.e.: more than the weight of rein), really only means that the rider is pulling.

Riders believe that if a young horse does not pull (or push) against the rein then the horse is not forward. The truth is, young horses can be forward and balanced without strong contact! The young horse can also be forward without kicking him in the belly and without being spurred. The leg aid is a learned process, meaning when the horse comes in from the field, leg pressure does not mean anything to him. Traditionally only the violent use of the whip makes him understand to go forward. We prefer the understanding that the little fly makes the big horse gallop in the field. *Let us be that little fly*. After lunging and work in-hand, the horse understands easily and clearly this concept. Lunging and work in-hand is a highly mental exercise. Visualization is the key.

The F. E. I. now promotes the so called "training pyramid" which says that steady contact must be sought. The problem is that this idea is in direct conflict with training happy athletes with invisible aids. How are you supposed to have *LIGHTNESS* with "contact," when contact has become more than the weight of steady reins and hand? Lightness is the absence of heavy contact, produced by the horse's self-carriage.

The pervasive belief is that the Dressage horse must be "driven into the contact." We see articles in national magazines about how many pounds, *POUNDS!* the rider must feel in his reins. Nationally recognized trainers espouse lifting weights in the gym to enable the riders arm muscles to carry the "contact" of a highly educated dressage horse. Connection between horse and rider has become confused with so called contact. What is constantly forgotten is that what the rider feels in the hands and muscles is what the poor horse feels on his very sensitive bars of his tender mouth, and in fact, all the way down his spine. The idea of contact has been convoluted from the idea of connection.

The tragedy of this misconception is that the potential relationship, communication and connection that horses may offer us is completely lost. Harmony is lost. Resistance is created as the horse tries, somehow, to cope with being told to *stop* and *go* at the same time! The dance we seek when we ride, hopefully, is destroyed. We might as well now get out our bicycle and ride it instead.

We are destroying our relationship with the horse because we are forcing the horse to do something physically. *In dancing, there is no force.*

The communication we seek disintegrates into pushing, driving, correcting, pulling. We no longer listen to our horse. This is not partnership; this is not communication.

Rollkur and aggressive behavior issues, are a consequence of mindless riding. It consists of forcing the horse's chin to its chest, producing blue tongues and pain all the way through the horse. This new technique was developed in the last few years, by Dutch and German trainers involved with high dollar investors in International competition. They were, and are, ready to sacrifice a great many horses in order to mechanize a few Grand Prix horses. Greed and disrespect of the horses has led to a multi-million-dollar industry. Not accepted by veterinarians and many judges, this technique is completely banned but still practiced and even taught to young riders. That is why we see so many horses completely over-bent. It is tragically becoming a normality. The judges are responsible. The permissiveness of the F. E. I. is responsible. We believe there are also many riders, trainers and judges that know better, yet very few speak up. We must all speak up and denounce this tragedy. Let's defend our horses, and speak up for them.

The visible relaxation of the lower jaw coming from self-carriage and lightness (deglutition) is a fundamental cornerstone that leads to *Descente de Main, Descente de Jambes*. Deglutition is the visible proof of the relaxation of the lower jaw. This is evidenced by the movement of the horse's mouth; the horse will salivate to varying degrees. The relaxation of the mouth, and jaw, the movement of the tongue are evidence of and related to the relaxed core of the horse. We hear talk of an engaged core but very recently I heard the term "prepared" core. The difference being that an engaged core is already in action, while the prepared core is ready to offer relaxed and supple movement The horse raises the bit in his mouth, and this translates to the whole of the horse in relaxation.

When you ignore this important piece of the puzzle, you have compromised the very nature of Dressage.

Self-carriage and lightness are interconnected. When self-carriage is absent then true lightness is impossible. When true self-carriage, meaning on the bit, and balanced, lightness comes from the rider.

F. E. I. Articles 403, 404, and 405 *all* state the horse must demonstrate clear self-carriage. How can this be possible when the horse must cope with the "contact" we impose on him? This very idea is so contradictory that it is laughable.

One of the goals of Dressage is to establish self-carriage. This means that the horse can easily, *comfortably* carry himself and his rider. This is what the words balance, harmony, and relaxation are all about. Trainers and riders toss the words about but very few have any real idea what they really mean and more importantly what they mean to the horse. The horse cannot find *comfort* when he is being made to endure pressure on his mouth and have his jaw clamped shut. The horse will do all he can to protect itself. Making himself as rigid as possible is an option. Keeping the haunches out behind his weight (the very opposite of collection) is another option. Tightening the neck is another option. All of these are attempts to escape the discomfort of "contact." We see *all* of these on a regular basis in International competitions today.

Dressage is supposed to help the horse feel balanced, relaxed, *free* to move and go forward under the rider. Contact shuts the horse down physically, mentally and emotionally.

Connection is a far, far better idea. Connection of the horse's back to its front end, connection of horse to rider and rider to horse.

Imagine for a moment how different horse and rider would feel it there was *connection* instead of *contact*. What joy!

The next time you ride your horse, ask yourself, what does my horse feel about this contact? Does my horse enjoy being driven into my hands? Is it improving his understanding? They are not stupid, insensitive beasts of burden. They are highly intuitive, extremely sensitive animals. The same horse that is required to endure a rider's legs squeezing, clamping, and banging, can feel a fly on his skin.

Descente de Main, Descente de Jambes is a French expression defining the feeling, the attitude, that we need no hands, no legs to ride our horse. We can sit quietly and think, picture, visualize, *be* with our horse. It is a letting go of our physical influence. It is the true connection of mind, body, and dare I say, heart. It is a state of no action. We become passive in our body, but not in our mind! The horse does not need our hand nor our legs to perform. He does need us to stay present with him.

A basic tenet of French Classical riding is each and every time we do less and less. Our horse understands more and more. When we arrive to the point of doing nearly nothing it is not enough. We need to put our hand and our leg into a position where they *cannot* act. At that very moment we have a change of consciousness....

*Joy and Freedom in Forward, with Fluidity. Navarone do Top ridden by Georgette Rubinstone.
Photo by Keron Psillas*

Soante in Piaffer, Mestre Nuno Oliveira

"This is the profound essence of the Art.

"This has never been thought of, explained or spoken of ever before. This is the gift that Dominique has delivered to the riding world.

"I can say on a personal level, that is a monumental gift, and has led to some of the most profound moments of my life. I also truly believe it has been the greatest gift to my horses. It is my profound wish that every rider could experience this."
—Liz Conrod

CHAPTER 5
THE GAITS

THE BASIS OF DRESSAGE IS THE PURITY OF THE GAITS.
THE WALK

F. E. I. ARTICLE 403 THE WALK 1 states:
"The walk is a marching pace in a regular and well-marked four (4) times beat with equal intervals between each beat. This regularity combined with full relaxation must be maintained throughout all walk movements."

The key idea of this article is that "full relaxation must be maintained."
    In order to produce a regular walk in full relaxation the horse needs to be happy and physically comfortable and feeling free.
    The acceptance of idea of strong contact of the hands, legs and seat produce a lack of flexibility which has a very negative impact on all the gaits, which is especially noticeable at the walk.
    Only mental comfort creates a good walk.
    A pure walk is four beats, is free and relaxed, even when the horse is collected. A compressed horse, heavy in hands with a driving seat and forcing leg will, most of the time, destroy the walk which then becomes lateral and short.

Interference from the rider and heavy aids disturbs the horse, and makes it difficult to maintain a good free walk. This is the gait where it is most obvious if the horse is not free and light. You can hide mental and physical problems more easily in trot and canter, but a quality walk cannot be maintained when we are heavy or have a forcing attitude. When he feels held and compressed, the horse cannot have a quality walk. It is obvious in most modern competition.

The walk is a very important gait. It is at the walk that the horse's level of relaxation can be clearly demonstrated. If a horse is tense, or mentally or physically uncomfortable it is very difficult to maintain the quality, the essence of the walk, which is 4 beats, regular, relaxed and ground covering. Regularity and cadence (4 beats) are quickly lost if the horse is not relaxed in mind and body.

It is for very good reason that F. E. I. Article 403 2 states: "irregularity, which might become an ambling movement, is a serious deterioration of the pace."

Even in collection the clear 4 beats must be maintained. When riders "push" or use a "driving" seat, the walk is often destroyed due to tension of the horse in the mouth, back and/or mind of the horse. An honest collected walk requires tact and lightness.

The F. E. I. states in article 403 3.2 for collected walk "showing a clear self-carriage, the head approaches the vertical position and *a light* contact is maintained with the mouth."

The important point is how do we define lightness. It is certainly not measured in pounds! The hands of the rider connect to the rein, and the rein connects to the most tender, fragile part of the horse's body, the bars of the mouth. So many riders forget that they are not holding reins; they are holding the horse's mouth, indeed the very nervous system and mind of the horse. We remind ourselves every day how we'd like to be touched if someone had a piece of metal running through our mouth. And make no mistake, horses are just as sensitive as people, perhaps even more so.

The walk that is compressed rather than collected becomes lateral and is no longer the pace defined in the F. E. I. rules. The reason that the walk was defined in article 403 was to protect and maintain the integrity and quality of the walk, in order to protect the horse. We repeat: Only mental comfort allows for a good walk.

The F. E. I. also states that in the collected, medium, extended and free walk "There should always be a clear difference in the attitude and over-tracking in these variations."

The F. E. I. states for the extended walk: "The Horse covers as much ground as possible, without haste and without losing the regularity of the steps. The hind feet touch the ground *clearly in front of the hoof prints of the fore feet*. The Athlete allows the horse to stretch out the head and neck forward and down."

This rule is no longer enforced at all.

Walk in lightness, Peaceful connection. Sedoso ridden by Cody Harrison. Photo by Katherine Howard

Even in extended walk, let alone collected walk, we see horses in competition badly over-bent, with bit pulled hard against the mouth, with neck bent in the middle vertebrae. We see horses' back legs lagging behind the croup. There is no freedom in the walk, no regularity, no impulsion. We will say in many international competitions the free walk is the *only* time during the test that we see horses at ease, even if only for few moments.

The F. E. I. states: "The free walk is a pace of relaxation in which the Horse is allowed complete freedom to lower and stretch out his head and neck. The degree of ground cover and length of strides, with hind feet stepping clearly in front of the footprints of the front feet, are essential to the quality of the free walk."

The free walk is included because if a horse has been forced into position when the rider is supposed to *let go* with the rein, (this is how we are supposed to demonstrate the 'free' walk), the horse will *not* stretch down because the back is *so* tense and rigid and the horse is trying desperately to protect its back and mouth, or he will run away.

"It is at the walk, under saddle, that a horse and rider can begin to have a quiet conversation, to clarify the intention for their time together. The rider has time to be sure to relax in her body, think about bent elbows coming to the side of the waist, opening her upper body, sitting tall with soft hips and thighs and allowing her lower legs to come into soft connection with her horse's sides. It is the time to connect the hand ever so softly with her horse's tender mouth. The horse gets to feel the weight of the rider without hurrying. Hopefully the horse and rider have already started this same conversation the moment the rider first came into contact with her horse that day, through grooming time, lunging, work in-hand and now this rider is sitting on her horse's back, it is time again to put the picture of how the conversation will be that day: to remember that this is time shared with someone you love and wish to have a loving dialogue and conversation with." Liz

THE TROT

The F. E. I. ARTICLE 404 THE TROT states:
"1. The trot is a two (2)-beat pace of alternate diagonal legs (left fore and right hind leg and vice versa) separated by a moment of suspension."
2. The trot should show free, active and regular steps.
3. The quality of the trot is judged by general impression, i.e. the regularity and elasticity of the steps, the cadence and impulsion in both collection and extension. This *quality* originates from a supple back and well-engaged hindquarters, and by the ability to maintain the same rhythm and natural balance with all variations of the trot."

The key word in this rule is "quality." As F. E. I. rules state, quality originates from a supple back, and well-engaged hind quarters. We have explained, in the last chapter, about the evils of contact, that the horse cannot, when ridden in strong contact, use his back properly and become supple. Suppleness only can come from relaxation.

Liz Conrod, Author Dancing in the Citronella Garden, Dancing in Harmony

When horses are tense and held in front, this produces a low-quality Spanish like trot. This mechanized modern so-called trot, is displayed in competition today. The tenseness also produces a pseudo passage like stride. The so-called suspension, that today's competitors display is again a false version of Trot. The desired true suspension that F. E. I. states we should be demonstrating, can only be obtained in relaxation and comes from true collection. The quality of suspension is the time spent off the ground in complete relaxation.

The big, extravagant floating trot in rigidity does not have true suspension. What we call suspension should be a balanced, supple, active, horse in Piaffe on the spot, or in Passage, staying suspended for the longer time in complete relaxation. The horse looks like a dancer, not an agitated military marcher in a parade.

What we see today is horses being forced to bounce about as they are being compressed by leg, hand and seat. The collected trot should show elevation but not suspension! The collected trot should not look like the Passage that covers ground. It should be engaged and show minimal suspension.

The exaggerated gait being asked for and rewarded today is not altogether far from the trots demanded from gaited horses. These are not natural gaits. We must remember Dressage should preserve the purity of the gaits not invent new, artificial ones.

This is a great misunderstanding. In the classical progression we go from trot, to collected trot, to school trot, to *doux* (soft) Passage and finally, Passage.

Because of the wrong assumption, that bigger gaits are more valued than more usual gaits, more and more dressage competition is rewarding breeds and breeding of horses that are bigger and have more "spectacular" looking gaits. This is due to trying to gain and impress audiences that know nothing of classical riding. Dressage is becoming a freak show. The huge giant movers showing exaggerated gaits are meant to attract paying customers. Then, when these horses are not even trained properly, we are demonstrating anti-classical principles.

The result does not allow the horse to use properly his hindquarters. It has been stated recently that we can have a "positive tension" which some justify as you can produce movements this way, in resistance. There is no such thing as "positive tension."

Let's be clear, Tension is Tension, produced by compression.

If the horse is compressed, rigidity can produce an artificial gait.

The competition trot we see so often today is an artificial gait. Dressage is about the purity of the gaits! It is so important not lose our classical knowledge and goals, in the name of modernity.

It is important to remember that the rules were put in place to protect the horses. When the F. E. I. rules are not respected and enforced then we have ceased to protect our horses.

Dom Fransisco was able to Piaffer, Extend and return to Piaffer in three strides.

3 strides later Forward, Supple, True Connection. Dom Fransisco ridden by Dominique Barbier, Photo by Marcia Hart

A quality trot is relaxed, round and with engaged hindquarters. The F. E. I. states that the trot must come from a supple back and well-engaged hindquarters. Many of the trots demonstrated today show a very exaggerated suspension in resistance, usually produced at the expense of the supple back. There is great emphasis now on the highly cadenced trot, which is often confused with actual collection. It is believed that if the trot shows elevation that you must have collection. Sadly, this is not necessarily true, as you can get a horse to demonstrate an exaggerated cadenced rhythm by making the horse rigid in his back, especially if the horse is forced into a heavy contact. Thus, we see horses so often in competition, today, with haunches disengaged, backs hollow, and showing cadence produced with rigidity, but not collection. Freedom is not often seen. The problems get much worse at the two extremes of the trot, in extension and in Piaffer.

The F. E. I. Article 404 4.5 Extended trot states:
"The fore feet should touch the ground on the spot towards which they are pointing."

This rule exists for the simple and very important reason that this protects the horse from being ridden in rigidity. When the toe of the horse is pointing far up and out in front of the horse, he cannot possibly put his foot down on that spot. This exaggerated flinging of the front legs is created by a very rigid and tight back. It is now prohibited in F. E. I. rules but still rewarded in the show ring. All engagement of the hindquarters is lost. This is especially evident in extended trot, where we see horses in Grand Prix tests showing an extended trot which does not even track up! The competitive trot seen in competition is a bastardized version of the Spanish trot and of the Passage ridden in complete rigidity and damaging to the horse in every stride.

The hoof pointed to where it lands rule is to insure the relaxation of the back and of the lower part of the neck, as well as and the correct proportional engagement of hind quarters.

This rule is disregarded at every level and in all international competition now. What is on display in competition today is no longer a correct trot. We now have leading professionals stating that this is ok as we now have the "modern" trot. The trot has not changed! It is ridiculous to say we have a new gait because we have destroyed the old one.

If this is what is rewarded in competition, then perhaps it is time to redefine it as "competition trot."

But if the F. E. I. and modern competition want to claim they are riding with classical principles, which remember *was* the founding goal of the F. E. I., then we need to teach and encourage our judges to use the correct criteria!

F. E. I. states; 4.5. Extended trot.
"The Horse covers as much ground as possible. Without hurrying, the steps are *lengthened to the*

utmost as a result of great impulsion from the hindquarters. The movement of the fore and hind legs should reach equally forward in the moment of extension."

Lengthening comes from collection. Lengthening leads to extension. The frame must be proportional to the stride. A long frame allows a long stride.

Farsista, in extension. Mestre Nuno Oliveira

We repeat: Hoof pointed to where it lands is to insure the relaxation and the correct proportional engagement of hind quarters.

The gait currently displayed is totally artificial and produced by tenseness in the neck and a whip, just like producing a Spanish gait.

The extended trots seen today do not even show an over-track, indeed rarely is the horse even tracking-up. The hind quarters are lagging behind the horse, necks are over-bent, backs are hollow. Horses are not allowed to lengthen their frames at all, they are merely made to throw forelegs out in front via driving legs and spurs.

This is a clear violation of F. E. I. rules yet is heavily rewarded in the show ring. Are judges not even aware of these rules? Why is this clear violation of rules that were meant to protect horses being ignored? Lengthening, and the ability to extend, comes from collection. The length of frame must be proportional to the length of stride. A long frame allows a long stride. Extended trot is supposed to be a long, ground covering trot! The exaggerated toe flipping, hind end trailing trots we see today in competition are not even trots anymore. The diagonalization that defines a correct trot is lost. The horse is prevented from using his own impulsion because his back is locked which is why we see pictures of "top" horses with haunches trailing out behind the horse. And the higher the level of competition the more this is seen. Then, to add insult to injury, we read in national dressage magazines that this is now the "modern" trot for today's horse. The horse is still a horse and the trot is still the trot. Remember the goal of the F. E. I. ? "To preserve and conserve purity for future competitors"? The higher up the horse gets, the more incorrect they are. We are going in the wrong direction! When collection has become compression and contraction, the horse is unable to extended, simply because his back has been locked and he is rigid. Now, in order to show something for an extension the horse is made to produce the exaggerated front-end movement. He can do little else. We do not see a 'happy athlete' in extended trot in competition.

THE CANTER

F. E. I. ARTICLE 405 THE CANTER states:
"1. The canter is a three (3)-beat pace where, in canter to the right, for example, the footfall is as follows: left hind, left diagonal (simultaneously left fore and right hind), right fore, followed by a moment of suspension with all four (4) feet in the air before the next stride begins.
2. The canter, always with light, cadenced and regular strides, should be moved into without hesitation.
3. The quality of the canter is judged by the general impression, i.e. the regularity and lightness of the steps and the uphill tendency and cadence originating from the acceptance of the bridle with a supple poll and in the engagement of the hindquarters with active hock action – and by the ability to maintain the same rhythm and a natural balance, even after a transition from one (1) canter to another. The Horse should always remain straight on straight lines and correctly bent on curved lines."

The quality of the canter is measured by a clear three beat gait with a very defined moment of suspension. The canter is a very special gait by the fact that you need a very defined balance for each movement. You have the canter, the counter canter, simple change, two-time tempi, one-time tempi and pirouettes. As trainers, we need to create the proper balance, especially for the canter. Each canter movement has its own proper balance and we must know what it is to help the horse to be correct. Only then is the horse able to give us the movement.

If we compress the canter, by demanding contact (more than the weight of the rein), we destroy the canter just as we destroy the walk. Compression is not collection. Having the horse on the bit and light, will facilitate roundness which is another hallmark of a quality canter. Engagement of the hind quarters is, of course, *key* and becomes more critical as we attain more collection. The very light inside rein is required to facilitate the engagement of the inside hind leg.

Considering that your correct position in canter is a passive position of haunches-in, the importance of positioning your outside elbow and hand is fundamental.

Your canter was established on the lunge on different size circles. For the *"basse ecole"* (the basic education of the young horse) the horse should be able to do a ten-meter circle in canter and counter canter.

This will help for your first flying change. Then we like to introduce the haunches-in at the canter in preparation for the flying change. The haunches-in allows the horse to sit on his haunches and keep the three-beat canter that is necessary for his pirouette.

As we can see in modern dressage the compression of the horse in canter destroys the very nature of the gait and leads to a four-beat canter. We have such an emphasis on flying changes that while many top competitors can demonstrate many flying changes, it is rare to see a good pirouette anymore. The reason we see many flying changes today is that they are better done with some degree of rigidity. The more changes you perform at once the more rigid the canter becomes. This is due to the fact that cumulative tempi changes cease to be an actual canter gait.

This is another instance where competition dressage should change its own rules since today's pirouettes are four beats, not three. Keeping the same rhythm in the canter, before and after the flying changes, and during the pirouette, demonstrates that a horse has correct training in canter. *No* change of rhythm should be seen in the pirouette.

Most often, we see pirouettes today that loose rhythm, become stuck, loose impulsion and are not on the spot. This is because true collection in three beats and lightness is very rare. Horses are not able to sit and maintain the balance and lightness to do a correct pirouette. Collection in canter is very rare, because todays canter is usually ridden in compression.

The F. E. I. states the canter *is* a 3-beat gait! This means that the horse will not have two hind feet (*nor* the two front feet) on the ground at the same time, as this automatically means the three beats have been lost.

The hallmark of canter work in Grand Prix tests today is the flying change. The majority of the canter time is spent in tempi changes. The very nature of the flying change invites the horse to be increasingly rigid, especially when tempi changes are asked over and over. With so many changes included in tests today it is not a surprise that a true three beat canter pirouette is very rare indeed.

Canter is THREE beats. Pirouette is a Canter Movement and must maintain THREE BEATS per F. E. I. rules. Sedoso ridden by Dominique Barbier. Photo by Keron Psillas

F.E.I. ARTICLE 413 THE PIROUETTE, THE HALF-PIROUETTE

In 413.6 The F. E. I. Clearly states: "In the pirouette or half-pirouette in canter, the Judges should be able to recognize a real canter stride although the feet of the diagonal – inside hind leg, outside front leg – are not touching the ground simultaneously."

Canter pirouette is supposed to be performed in a three-beat canter. The rules clearly state this. Yet judges today often reward clearly four beat pirouettes, and even a so-called pirouette where the canter is lost entirely. When was the last time anyone saw a true three beat pirouette in International Competition?

Pirouette Right in correct three beat Canter in Descente de Main.
Saramago do Top ridden by Candida von Braun. Photo by Keron Psillas

The canter, like the walk, shows the purity of the gait when it is well performed. Canter can also demonstrate the problems created by incorrect training. It is easier to disguise the trot badly ridden with training a horse in compression, imposing heavy contact. The nature of the trot makes it possible to fake it. The walk and the canter are so easily destroyed by mental or physical discomfort that these are the gaits where true collection and good training are proven.

CHAPTER 6
THE IMPORTANCE OF THE FOUR TRACK SHOULDER-IN

François Robichon de La Guérinière said that the Shoulder-in was the first and last lesson he taught to every horse.

Horses shoulders are not connected in the same fashion as ours; he has no collarbone and the shoulder is entirely connected to the horse through muscles, ligaments and tendons. The shoulders have no boney connection with the rest of the skeleton.

Lunging is very important for *all* horses, Of course when we speak of lunging, we mean that the horse is on the bit, round, the horse is bent in the direction of the circle and he can walk, trot, and canter calmly and freely forward and relaxed.

When you lunge it is *critical* the corner of the mouth (the bit) be in horizontal line with of the point of the shoulder. The side reins must be adjusted to allow this. Placed low so that they cross the point of the shoulder, parallel to the ground and adjusted so they allow the bend we are asking for, usually a bit shorter on the inside and *longer* on the outside.

All horses are able to relax their back when they are in this position, or lower. All horses should be able to be and stay in this position. If they are not, they are not ready to carry a rider!

Correct lunging in perfect position on his own. When the back is round the horse can carry himself correctly. Bailado do Top Photo by Sarah Southwell

    We must clarify between riding long and low and the horse being able to be long and low. There is confusion in a lot of people's minds about this idea. The horse should be able to *be* long and low, meaning the horse should be able to relax and stretch his back. This does not mean he should be ridden in this position. The balance when the rider is on the horse is very different.

    The same with work in-hand, the horse should be able to cross his legs when his neck is long and low. This is not how we ride the Shoulder-In, again because the balance is totally different with the rider on top.

The work in-hand is how we prepare for the true Shoulder-In. The true four track Shoulder-In that can prepare the horse for the piaffer or an extension.

Work In-Hand is an important part of the conversation with your horse, and allows the start of a deeper connection., Sedoso with Dominique Barbier Photo by Keron Psillas

The goal of the four-track shoulder-in is to help relax the horse and help him become more supple, and allow correct bending to the inside without the inside rein. This allows the inside hind leg to cross under the body of the horse, which *is* the correct understanding of collection. This means the lowering of the haunches and *therefore* the lightening of the front end. This is why we do *not* artificially raise the front end. This is in direct opposition with the F. E. I. required three track shoulder-in ridden in contact, which guarantees rigidity in the horse.

Paying extreme attention to the emotional state of your horse is primordial to the success of the Shoulder-In. Only when the horse *feels* good can he give you his best Shoulder-In.

Perfect Horse, Shoulder-In in lightness, leading to the Descente de Main, Descente de Jambes Herodes Alentejo ridden by Debra Barbier. Photo by Keron Psillas

The work in-hand is sometimes necessary before lunging because sometimes this is the way to show the horse the position that he can have for lunging. He can find his position of comfort, physical, mental and emotional. As we know, it will be a different position on the left and the right. The horse will be able to relax his lower jaw when he reaches this basic position. Try to keep him talking, in "deglutition." If he remains in this state, he will let you know that he is happy, relaxed and working. Later we will vary the energy.

Horses often have tight and stiff shoulders. When the rider then takes contact and pulls and kicks to try to go sideways, the shoulders become even tighter, and the horse gets more physically and mentally stressed, leading to one or both shoulders being blocked. This is very common, and the solution is to practice the Shoulder-In to alleviate this stress and stiffness.

Of course, this Shoulder-In is given to the horse as a position. It is not the action that was caused by the pulling rein and kicking leg, which contributed to the problem in the first place.

A Perfect Moment. Ultraje VO ridden by Melinda d'Amico. Photo by Debra Barbier

The great gift of the shoulder-in position is that the horse can begin to soften all the connective tendons due to the circular motion of crossing his legs. The opening and closing of the shoulders, opens the energy, allowing softness all along the horse's spine and back. Therefore, the bigger the crossing, the greater the suppleness the horse is able to achieve.

When we position the horse in Shoulder-In position, he is able to start to loosen the shoulders. The position of the Shoulder-In offers the horse the first feeling of carrying weight more towards his hind end (haunches), the beginning of the feeling of the horse carrying his head (and the rider) by sitting back. This is where true collection begins. Balance, collection and lightness are all intertwined. Please remember that the Shoulder-In is for riding in the walk and trot only. Do not place your horse in Shoulder-In in canter. This is because, in fact, the rider's position is one of passive Haunches-In so that the rider can be in position *with the horse* for the canter. Shoulder-In can lock the horses canter, making balance very difficult and causing discomfort

The position of Shoulder-In enables the horse to begin to understand how to carry himself more comfortably under the rider. Collection is now gained by position, in lightness and balance.

This is a far cry from the so-called collection obtained by "driving the horse into the contact." By practicing four-track shoulder-in, haunches-in and pirouette, you are building the foundation for your horse's true balance in self-carriage and relaxation and for all of the higher-level movements.

In the 1963 version of the F. E. I. rules, Article 410 states that the inside legs pass and cross in front of the outside legs. The understanding here is that we want a four-track shoulder-in and that the Shoulder-In is a crossing movement. Of course, this makes sense since it is a suppling exercise. The later versions that define the three-track Shoulder-In led us down the wrong path. Any feeling rider that has had the experience of a Shoulder-In that improved the walk or trot. It was a four track Shoulder-In.

When the horse is in a four-track Shoulder-In, he can begin to relax the muscles and ligaments that connect the shoulders. (Imagine how you feel when your shoulders are drawn up and tight. How does your neck feel? How does your back feel?) This allows for much greater relaxation all along the spine. It is like opening the door to allow the flow of energy from the back legs, up to the front, connecting the whole horse. The common three track Shoulder-In practiced today does very little to help the horse become supple. We want him to feel more and more supple, balanced and light. We do not supple the horse. We need to position him so *he* can be more supple!

By practicing your four-track Shoulder-In, your Haunches-In and your Pirouette, you are building the foundation for your horse's true balance in self-carriage and relaxation and for all of the higher-level movements.

THE 'NEW' SHOULDER-IN, UNDERSTANDING THE OLD ONE.

The New Shoulder-In. It is in fact, a rediscovery of the old true four track Shoulder-In that leads the horse to suppleness. Sedoso ridden by Dominique Barbier. Photo by Keron Psillas

Shoulder-In has been practiced for a very long time. La Guérinière said it was the first and the last lesson. We use the word "biomechanics" these days, which is an oxymoron as the shoulder is not connected by bone to the horse. Only muscles, tendons and ligaments connect the shoulder to the body. Therefore, this is primordial that we understand how the shoulders function. Even more important, the mental and emotional well-being of our horse, is connected to his ability and willingness to give us his ultimate Shoulder-In.

*The most important aspect of the Shoulder-In is to consider the emotional state of the horse. This is when he is **comfortable** and free of all worries. Only when it is close to perfect, the horse is able to give us his back, allow his hind leg to go underneath him and free the shoulders to the best of his ability.*

Shoulder-In should be called "Shoulders In." That best describes the position needed for a four track Shoulder-In.

Horses often start with blockage in one or both shoulders, generally coming from a weak or non-functioning back. This is often produced by strong contact in the wrong position, made worse by forcing the movement.

When the back and hind legs do not function correctly, the horse is not able to carry the weight on his back legs. Then the weight is transferred to the shoulders and limit their movement. A good Shoulder-In improves the regularity of the crossing of both hind legs, and allows the inside hind leg to cross under the body. This, in turn, allows the energy of the back legs to go *through* free shoulders, withers, neck, jaw. Now the horse is able to go *forward*.

When the back relaxes, it will become clearer which shoulder or shoulders need attention. So, while we call this movement the Shoulder-In it is about the position of the shoulders taking an inside track relative to the haunches. Movement in this position allows the back to work, become stronger and makes it easier for the horse to carry us.

Any conscious trainer or rider who feels his horse, knows that when his horse is happy everything goes well. Any forcing will "kill the bubble." Harmony is destroyed. A thinking rider knows that a rigid three track Shoulder-In is as useless as a rigid half pass. The question is: Is your horse better, more supple after the three track Shoulder-In? Please, when you ride ask your horse, your partner "How does he feel"? This should be your daily question. Is my horse happy? It is the question for your dance partner. If you want to dance, take care of your partner. He is the *dancer*.

As we lunge, work in-hand, and ride in Shoulder-In and Haunches-in, be looking for the "deglutition." This is important because it is the visual expression of his well-being. Deglutition is the result of relaxation of the lower jaw. Deglutition is the lifting of the bit by the tongue. The importance of the tongue is the connection to the core, the center. We want the horse to have a little "murmur," not to be mute in his mouth and jaw. *Un leger murmure,* is French for a "little quiet voice."

We get mute horses when we insist on "contact."

From the toes to the tongue, Deglutition is the togetherness of the body and mind, very similar to the sense you get in yoga practice where you have to put your tongue at the top of your palette, where the human core is very similar to the horse.

Please reference the article appendixes at the end of book.

The smallest change in angle can produce anxiety. Every horse has his own position, amount of angle, and amount of energy that he can give you the best crossing. Each day the rider must seek this ideal. Sometimes it can change day to day. What is important is that the Shoulder-In is an ever-changing position and not something you impose upon the horse. You must find the position in which the horse can give you his best Shoulder-In, the maximum of crossing he can achieve that day.

SOME PROBLEMS CAN ARISE IF:
- NO CLEAR VISUALIZATION OF THE MOVEMENT: remember the picture of your horse crossing in the work in-hand.
- NO CLEAR POSITIONING: Plan ahead. Positioning is the first step of a small circle or corner.
- HORSE NOT ON THE BIT, HORSE IS NOT IN THE LISTENING POSITION: Remember the position you had when the horse was on the lunge line. If that was not confirmed you may need to go back to lunge line.
- WRONG BALANCE, NOT LIGHT: Shorten the reins, check *your* position, and start to play with your fingers.
- TOO MUCH OR TOO LITTLE ANGLE: You are looking for the same angle you had in work in-hand. The horse told you which angle he likes!
- EXCESSIVE USE OF RIDER'S INSIDE LEG: Remember you are not forcing or pushing the horse sideways. You are positioning him to be able to cross his legs.
- PULLING ON INSIDE REIN, USING HAND FOR DIRECTION: Be sure your inside rein is short enough to position him and then put your inside hand *on the saddle* so that it does not move. Look where you are going.
- TOO LITTLE OR TOO MUCH IMPULSION: You have learned with the lunging the correct amount of energy in relaxation. Picture that.
- TOO FAST OR SLOW RHYTHM: Play the music of the dance. Count the rhythm when you lunge and repeat that in the saddle. The music contains the energy of the dance.
- TOO MUCH EMPHASIS ON SIDEWAYS VERSUS FORWARD: When you keep the rhythm, you keep the flow. All movements must be forward. Think about the log floating down the river.
- RIGID BACK FOR RIDER LIMITS THE MOVEMENT OF THE HORSE: Relax your lower back and allow your hips, and belly to go with the horse. Be the centaur. Your back and the horse's back are one.
- DOING TOO MUCH: Picture your horse. Again, picture the log going down the river. Kicking the log, pulling on it, will not be any help. Practice doing less and then the horse can give you more.

Help the beginner rider by working the horse in-hand with rider on top.

In the desired Shoulder-In, we will find the relaxation for the lower jaw. The delightful *"le leger murmure"* that indicates the perfect well-being of the horse. Now you can have close to perfect communication with your partner. Your goal is the Shoulder-In in *descente de main, descente de jambes. These* are the classical principles that the F. E. I. should defend and uphold.

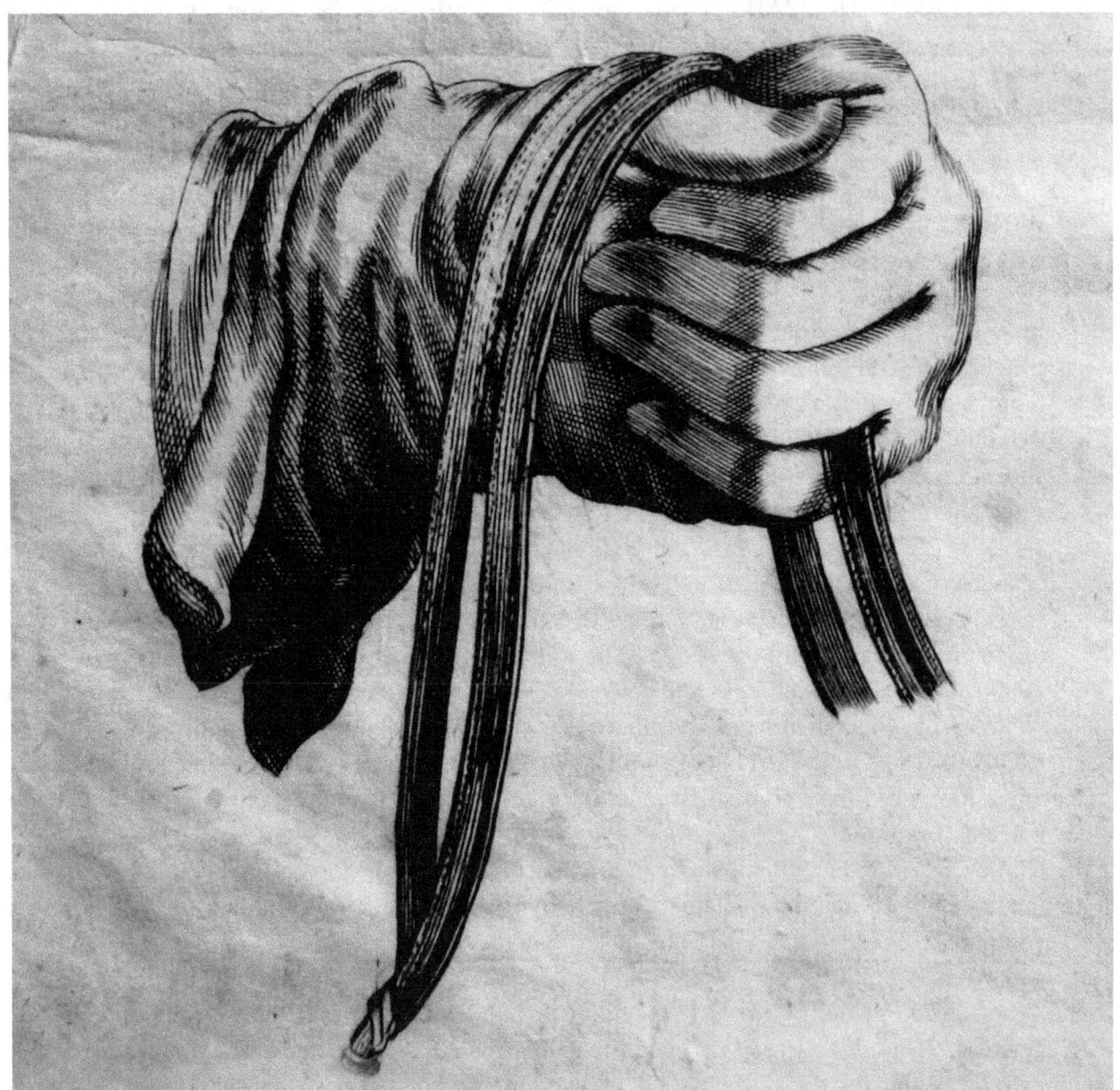

See the compassion, love, and feel the softness. The hands must always communicate in the gentlest way.
Photo is from the book by Georg Simon Winters published in 1678

Relaxation in Position Practice "Position- No Action." Ultraje VO ridden by Dominique Barbier. Photo by Keron Psillas

Paying attention to the upper part of the body is paramount. It must be back and upwards, with a consciousness of the elbow connection to the waist. This results in hands being a bit higher and much lighter. Sometimes it is necessary to have too much temporary bend in the neck. It can help. Sometimes also slight opening of the inside rein *position* can be helpful. This does not mean we act with the inside rein. We want to always think *"Position, NO Action."* We must not create inside rein contact. Even if in open position the rein must be passive and giving. The inside rein contact kills the horse's ability and willingness to put his inside leg under himself, which is our very goal.

The rider must be waiting for the "let go" of the back of the horse. This results in 2 to 8 inches of the improvement of the length of the stride in relaxation. True relaxation in the stride is always better than forcing or "driving" (a term than should be reserved for cows and cars) with legs, back and spurs.

The rider must be able to physically relax his own body, especially his legs. If you notice how human legs are attached there is little space to accommodate the round barrel of our horse. This means we must be able to *relax* our thighs to allow the lower leg to lie on our horse. It is only when the rider's lower leg can be in soft connection with our horse, like a wet (or even dry!) towel that we can have the finesse to talk to our horse. We hear that we must drive with the leg, when in fact we should whisper with the leg, if needed, for a brief moment. The leg is like the hand of the great dancer. Invites but never demands. Many riders need to do physical work of their own to allow this flexibility in their own bodies. This is a far cry from articles we read about lifting weights to be able to ride well. We are asking our horse to improve his range of motion and we must ask the same of ourselves.

As we stated at the beginning of this chapter, Shoulder-In is the first and last exercise.

In conclusion, the Shoulder-In, is the most important exercise. It is fundamental throughout the entire life and training process, at every level. Nearly every problem or issue that can arise throughout the horse's life is directly related to this exercise.

It is of utmost importance that our horse loves his Shoulder-In at all levels. A relaxed mental and emotional state of the horse is essential for the best Shoulder-In. Conversely, if your Shoulder-In is not truly excellent, there is a very good chance that you did not pay enough attention to the emotional well-being of your partner.

CHAPTER 7
THE WAY FORWARD

CREATING THE CONTEXT OF THE ERA

In order to understand and to move forward, we need to know what the world situation is. Globalization is a fact of life for us now. A lot of traditional ways of thinking are being challenged, both good and bad.

Our fast-paced modern world is demanding instant results and gratification.

Very few people spend any time reading or learning about the "old Masters." This is most unfortunate as there is a vast pool of knowledge available that is not being honored or used. This is not to say that all old methods are necessarily good, but are worth while studying.

Study of the horse is very important. Horses have not changed. Our perception of what and who they are has changed. Again, some for the better, some not.

It is important to realize when people speak of the "modern" horse, the "modern gaits" that they are ignoring knowledge and history, and horses' basic nature.

In the horse world, very few people seem to be interested in the *process* of training. They want to go to the horse show and present a horse that can win. The two different approaches lead to very different results.

When we train for the horse's education, there is a progression of understanding that is often abandoned in preparing the horse to ride a test.

Conversely, in our modern world we have a much greater awareness of our personal heath, environmental health and the health of our animals.

The scientific world has brought us a lot of new ideas for how to take better care for our animals. We are learning how to be aware of the animal world with a greater understanding and connection. When we apply this to horses, hopefully, we are becoming aware of communicating with them on a level that has not been approached before. Horses have long been perceived as beasts of burden that are not very smart and need to be dominated.

A more enlightened and true idea is that they, in fact are highly sensitive, and very intuitive beings.

For instance, we are now aware now that horses can have ulcers. They experience true stress when they do not understand or trust what is expected from them or when they are not treated justly.

A WORLD APPROACH FOR THE WAY FORWARD

We have spoken out a lot in previous chapters about the negative trends in competitive Dressage today.

Now, we would like to focus on how to go forward.

First, we must decide if, indeed, we want to change direction.

One option is to change the rules for competition. But that choice needs to be open, conscious and intentional. If we simply let the status quo become the accepted norm, then truly we are making a decision that competitive Dressage no longer has any relationship to Classical principles and we are creating a whole new type of "Dressage." If that is to be the case, we will now have "Sport Dressage."

This is a major and permanent step.

An alternative, today, is to commit to educating judges, trainers, riders, and even audiences about Classical principle's, rules and ethics.

If the F. E. I. wants to reward the 'show trot' and the four-beat canter pirouette, then they need to define those movements so that 'Sport Dressage' would have a new definition, and a clear way to be judged.

We must decide if we will apply the rules as the F. E. I. has written them, or change the rules.

What is happening today in the competitive world is riders, trainers and judges are masquerading as if they are following the F. E. I. mission.

The F. E. I.'s rules are very good ones, and were put in place by visionary horsemen to protect horses. They knew that competing could compromise horses, horsemanship and principles. They knew that one school's value system could overtake another.

The F. E. I. founders meant to keep the balance with their rules. Indeed today, the German school's values have become the overriding guidelines of competition. Precision, obedience, and submission are paramount in today's show ring. We even have German words now in F. E. I. rules that have no clear translation. The more French school's values of Lightness, harmony, partnership and beauty have fallen away as far less important.

So, we have lost the balance.

As in all cases, when we lose balance, we must come back toward our center.

What steps can we take to reverse the trend of incorrect training being rewarded, and therefore becoming normalized?

Judges need to be able to understand, apply and enforce the rules. This means that judges must have the education, integrity and authority to carry out the F. E. I.'s mission, which is the Happy Athlete!

We need to teach and remind judges of the concept of relationship, in which no force, no aggression, is allowed in any form.

Judges need to witness and reward harmony.

Riders and horses enjoying the dance, showing self-carriage in forward movement, must be recognized and rewarded with appropriate scores.

The horse moving on his own in lightness is a demonstration of beauty.

We must ask the F. E. I. to eliminate the verbiage that allows over-bending "for a period of time"! How many minutes is it OK to hurt our horses before they perform a test for us?

We admit there are many that say we have gone too far down the road. They believe the F. E. I. has lost the ability to control the competitive world. We say the F. E. I. needs our support and voices to encourage them to follow their mission.

Stewards must be empowered and educated enough to enforce the rules. We could have Judges in the warm up arenas as well, to issue warnings and sanctions when warnings are not heeded.

Stewards must recognize Rollkur and riders over-bending their horses.

They must be taught and expected to enforce rules about overly tight nose bands, most especially the "crank" style.

We must enforce the rules about tack, especially bridles and nosebands, which are much too tight.

It would be a great idea to have judges and or veterinarians on the grounds to help the stewards with enforcement.

Show organizers and riders need to understand that the public and the sponsors are watching and recognize abuse when they see it.

The mechanized robot-like horses are not what we want.

The new so-called "Leg Mover"- Non Classical training leads to disconnected movement. Horses have not changed the way they move.

Today we have really fabulous horses such as, Totilas and Fuego, among many others that have great abilities. Sadly, they are incorrectly trained and look like freaks of nature. This is not Dressage. Education is paramount. Imagine, if you can, what these exceptional horses would look like if they were ridden classically in true collection and lightness.

The sponsors must realize that the public is aware of the truth and the consequences will tarnish the sponsors image and hurt their sales.

Kip Mistral asked Michel Henriquet:
Can equestrian art (classical equitation) be successfully combined with competition dressage (contemporary equitation)? Michel answered:
"*No.* Master Nuno Oliveira considered that it was impossible to reconcile the classical equitation, meaning the equitation of the School of Versailles, with the modern dressage." "And I think the same thing." He said.

Michel Henriquet said his wife Olympic French team rider, Catherine Durand was pretending that she was not following in the tradition of centuries of master teachers of classical equitation who so prized this lightness as a symbol of the subtlety possible in the relationship between horse and human. Instead she actually *simulated* the strong contact with the horse that the judges expect to see today in contemporary equitation.

We find the following statements on the F. E. I.'s web site:

F. E. I. Value Statement:

As an organization and a governing body, we are passionate about our sport. We celebrate the unique bond between horse and human (#TwoHearts)

> **HORSE FIRST** The welfare of the horse is our top priority.

> **PERFORM AS ONE** A unique sporting partnership built on mutual trust and respect.

> **FAIR AND EQUAL** A universal and level playing field for men and women of all ages to compete together from grassroots to the world stage.

> **FOR TODAY AND TOMORROW** Meeting the needs of today without compromising tomorrow.

These are wonderful statements and this is the very path we need to pursue.

We will not change the course we are on unless people speak up.

We vote with our dollar. When we attend a horse show and an obviously tense, frightened horse wins, we need to publicly ask why. Dressage is looking for spectators. The spectators are watching and should raise their concerns to show officials responsible for the well-being of the horses.

We need the F. E. I. and show organizers to understand that they are losing a huge audience. We do honestly believe that there are many people worldwide that have written off competitive Dressage, as they should.

We need to allow competitors to be judged on merit and not fashion.

We need to ask the F. E. I. to enforce their own rules! We need to support the F. E. I. in enforcing their own rules, as well.

We need brave trainers and judges to speak up when they see abusive training at shows or anywhere. We need to include education about Classical principles taught at judge's forums, clinics etc. We understand this will not be easy as there are fewer and fewer trainers with the knowledge available. But we do know that there are trainers throughout the world that no longer participate due to conscience.

We have spoken to many people that do not believe we can integrate Classical and competitive Dressage, they are too far apart now, and the two communities cannot be reconciled. We are not ready to accept this. But we must take steps now, or it will indeed be too late.

The Personal Journey Forward

The next generation of trainers, and riders is faced with many challenges of how to proceed.

We are in an era in which each individual must decide why they ride, how they train and how they will treat their horses. They must choose what they want the relationship to feel and look like.

It is our personal belief (prayer) that Dressage competitors do love their horses. No little girl or boy starts out riding horses to go and win ribbons and championships. This does however, become part of the dream, for many, and can lead down the wrong path for the horses. We can certainly compete and stay true to Classical principles, but honestly it is very unlikely that this will lead to success in the show ring. Especially today when the classically ridden horse is so very rarely rewarded. So, if a rider wants to continue to show they need a very clear idea of why they do so, and cannot be disappointed with results. You can carefully select some knowledgeable judges that can offer comments that can help you.

Certainly, there are people attracted to horses because their personality is drawn to mastering, controlling and dominating. But for most, it is love, passion, beauty that draws us to horses initially.

We need to keep compassion in mind so that we do not lose our way. Always keep in mind that you can and should look for coaches, trainers and clinicians that align with your core values.

We are suspicious that there are trainers and riders in competition today that do not approve of standards being adopted now, but do not speak up for fear of reprisal.

"We ride as we are."
—Dominique Barbier

BROKEN OR BEAUTIFUL

Connection in partnership. Love your horse, listen to him, honor him.
Larapio Coimbra with Dominique Barbier Photo by Keron Psillas

Every day, ask yourself, did I dance today, did my horse dance with me? Be as honest as you can with your answer. Further ask your horse. He will tell you, if you listen.

"As a picture is worth a thousand words" the example you portray with your horse will speak volumes to your community.

We are setting the example for future riders. Honor your horse. Esquilo DC ridden by Brooke Hurst

It is difficult sometimes, to stay loyal to what you believe when all those around you are doing otherwise, but if we do not do that, then we compromise the principles. Self-discipline is the key. We can all learn, certainly, but never compromise your horse to gain the approval of anyone.

For your personal education, you must take the time and make an effort to read the fundamentals of the Classical approach by the Masters.

These authors include but are not limited to, François Robichon de la Guérinière (1688-1751), François Baucher (1796-1873, Gustav Steinbrecht (1808-1885), Mestre Nuno Oliveira (1925-1989), and Dom Diogo de Bragança marques de Marialva (1930-2012). This is not a complete list by any means, but these authors cover the essence of classical methods.

Please see our recommended reading list at the end of this book.

In the era that the Masters were writing, they were involved in what we term *physical riding*.

The mental aspect of thinking and communication had not yet been thought of nor imagined.

Stay connected to yourself and your horse. Ben Hur Do Retiro ridden by Anne Douard Palmer.
Photo by Marcia Lewis

Today we understand that there are multiple layers of communication and we now know that visualization is a powerful and effective tool. There are many books now about using visualization in sports and activities, from skiing, golfing, soccer etc. We are learning it is also an incredible tool to communicate with people and animals, including horses.

In the Classical progression today, we use mental riding, meaning being present and using visualization. This better allows us to be aware of the emotional well-being of our horses. It significantly contributes to the connection that we are seeking with our horses. When we are together and one with our horse, we become true partners.

"This may sound like pie in the sky, but I, for one, have honestly and truly experienced this more times that can be counted. I have experienced my thought becoming my horse's thought and action, even before I knew I was thinking of a movement. The mind connection becomes instantaneous. It is true, it is real. It is the most incredible gift that we can share with our horses." - Liz

Be very careful, the word *Classical* has been exploited. Very few people have had a chance to know and work under a Master *Ecuyer*. There are many books out today that are deceitful. Ask your coach, which you choose carefully. Your coach should be able to clarify and explain anything that you question, and it should make sense in your heart.

The Native American people say, we do not learn, we "Remember." Truth has always been truth. The *"Basse Ecole"* (basic simple principles), apply today as they always have and we need to keep them in mind now as much as ever, in preparation for more collected *"Haute Ecole"* work.

First of all, we need to establish the basic relationship with our horse through proper lunging and work in-hand. (see: *Dressage for the New Age*) This is a fundamental first step.

When riding, start with the walk and the Shoulder-In, then Haunches-In and Pirouette. When these are well established and calmly done, the trot Shoulder-In, then Haunches -In, can be practiced.

When your walk and trot Shoulder-In and Haunches-In are correctly done and your horse is comfortable, then your horse is considered "trained" and ready for the high school. If you short cut this work, all of the rest of your work will be incorrect. Any later problems that you encounter, come from the fact of a lack of quality of these movements. This is exactly what is meant when you hear the expression "you must return to the basics" when you have problems.

> "The Shoulder-In is the first and last lesson to be given to the horse."
> "Shoulder-In is the alpha and the omega of all exercises."
> "This exercise is the most difficult and the most useful of all of those which must be used to supple the horse."
> —François Robichon de la Guérinière
>
> "Shoulder-In is the aspirin of horseback riding. It cures everything."
> —Mestre Nuno Oliveira

In order to keep and pursue harmony with your horse we advise that you study and practice the Classical approach, even if you are interested in competing.

> Dominique always says the definition of Classical Dressage,
> "is to enjoy the communication and the feel between two beings
> and to express it as a beautiful dance."

If you can keep this in mind, as you proceed on your journey with your horse, you will find it easier to avoid going down the path of hard contact and compression.

As we mentioned before, Michel Henriquet was a French classical *Ecuyer*. His wife, Catherine Durand, was interested in competing, and in fact was chosen for the French team for the 1992 Barcelona Olympic Games. She competed with Orphée, the first Lusitano ever to compete in the Olympics.

As Michel Henriquet said, Catherine had to fake strong contact for the competition but never worked this way at home. She trained classically but would show her horse in a different light, to appear to comply with what judges seemed to want to see. This is a unique successful example of an individual trying to reconcile the two worlds.

We have some associations and groups now that are starting to speak out about the problems we are having. Xenophon Group in Germany, Allege Ideal in France, Classical Riding in England, Equitazione Sentimentale in Italy have the same concerns.

These associations are the result of members being concerned with what is seen today and being represented as Dressage. They respect and want to preserve Classical values.

These well-intentioned groups will hopefully, gain in influence and effectively work to preserve Classical principles without compromise.

We have seen petitions that have been signed by thousands of people protesting the treatment of horses seen in top level dressage competition.

We do need to keep the focus on exposing abuse (Rollkur, Blue Tongue Syndrome, dehydrated horses etc.) and making it known that this is unacceptable.

There is a growing movement, at the grass roots level, of people that are searching for a different relationship with their horses.

We can embrace this trend, and we can go forward together or we can continue the splintering of philosophies between Classical and Competitive Dressage.

The F. E. I. and horse show organizers say they want to build audiences. Indeed, the tiny community of the horse show world could expand these audiences with the showing of horses that display the happiness and joy through the Happy Athlete.

As well, if competition was viewed as educational, and in the best interest of horses, judged by properly educated judges, show organizers may well find they attract many more competitors.

The F. E. I. had to amend the rules to include the code of conduct in our recent era. It did not need to be mentioned in the first rules, as at that time, competitors were presumed to be horse people.

The joy and the pleasure to share a dance with your partner, the happiness that comes with it, the beauty, is the meaning and goal of real Dressage. That is what we have to share with the world.

Because there is a basic non-understanding of the rules, and how they affect the horse we need some better training tools.

One unique idea is to create DVD's of an animated horse that shows exactly what happens when a horse is correct. The DVD would demonstrate exactly what the horse looks like when the rules are applied and what is happening to the horse when the rules are not applied. The DVD would demonstrate the required movements, and the reasoning behind why movements should look a particular way.

We need a definitive visual aid for people to be educated as to what is correct. We need to show clearly what the gaits are, what the position of "on the bit" is. We need to show the relationship of the *Ramener* (head and neck position) and the engagement of the hind quarters in order to produce correct collection in lightness. We need to show exactly what different levels of collection look like in lightness versus compression with heavy contact. This would be the perfect tool to see how to create different balances that allow the movement to happen.

The DVD would demonstrate the qualities of correct movements and the defects of incorrect movements and would help the judges to correctly apply the scale of the scores.

After the Olympics, Dominique said the following words, "At the Olympics… most of the movements were not correct." "What is very sad is that I am not sure if the perfect horse had come into the ring at the Olympics the judges would have recognized it." But this quote isn't referring to any recent competition. Rather, it was published in the April 1977 issue of Dressage & CT in referring to the 1976 Bromont, Canada Olympic Games. At that time, there were concerns of flashy show trots and four beat canter pirouettes. Forty-four years later, these sentiments still ring true.

Nervous energy creates physical and mental rigidity. We believe the untold truth about modern Dressage, is that training is now done by using resistance and rigidity.

See the appendix for the entire article.

We often forget, or never recognized at all, that horses are sensitive, highly intelligent beings. They have moods, physical difficulties, past experiences, and feelings. They have excellent memories. Horse cannot speak in our human language. Therefore, when our horse resists they are using the only means they have to communicate back to us! If we don't listen to them, then we are imposing our will without justice and without any real communication.

Rider & Trainer must always work together for the benefit and well-being of the horse. Xamado do Top ridden by Davi Carrano. Photo by Keron Psillas

If you train your horse with the attitude that they can, and will talk with us, if we can remember to talk with them, then we can develop an honest partnership in communication.

When we push and drive our horse forward, because we think he is too stupid to go forward on his own, we are not communicating.

Yet, if we make ourselves understood and allow the horse to participate, the majority of the time the horse will do his best. If he does not, it behooves you, to figure out why not!

Horses are generous and very honest animals. They are always present in the moment. If we treat them as something to be dominated, controlled, mastered, or to be fought with, then there is no room for partnership.

Leave the idea of "driving" to your car, which is a machine. Horses are not machines.

We write this today on Memorial Day. It is our earnest hope that 50 years from now we do not look back at a lost art, and lost knowledge.

We sincerely hope that horses at Dressage shows, especially at the top level are ridden in lightness, harmony and joy for them and the riders. We hope that these Dressage principles are taught, valued and practiced by an ever-growing community worldwide. For the horses' sake, and ours.

The knowledge exists. Horses are horses. We must keep the best traditions. Rider Jose Athaide

Below, we have included the most frequently asked questions, asked repeatedly at clinics, and at our symposiums held twice a year at Barbier Farm, each spring and fall.

TO DOMINIQUE: At this point do you believe we can reconcile Competitive Dressage with Classical Dressage?

DB Well, this is my great hope. But we must take strong action now. The very small group of people in the world today that are representing "Dressage" at the International level will need to make a decision, a commitment to learn, practice and maintain classical principles. It may well be that they are forced to change by the majority of other horse people.

TO DOMINIQUE: What steps can individuals take at this time?

We can set a goal, get educated, choose a trainer in harmony with your beliefs, and practice compassion with your horse.

TO DOMINIQUE: What is the most important classical principle?

This is to have your partner happy! This is the old F. E. I. Happy Athlete. We can translate that to mean make your horse comfortable physically and mentally. Do your best to make yourself understood and do not disturb him. François Baucher said "make yourself understood and let it happen" This is the only way that your horse, your dance partner, can express himself. This is the most important preoccupation of the *Ecuyer*, the true horseman.

TO DOMINIQUE: How do we quantify Beauty?

Well, it is not a matter of quantification. It is a matter how we can be in a space of appreciation. Beauty is everywhere and in everything. It is simply the way we look at things. We need to take time to breathe and to look. The reason that beauty is not often seen in modern Dressage is that precision is placed above the dance. When we see beauty, we feel joy.

"Joy is the infallible sign of the presence of God" Teilhard de Chardin

TO DOMINIQUE: Why is it that the relaxation of the lower jaw is such a pillar of classical training? What is important about the lower jaw being relaxed?

When the horse relaxes his lower jaw and chews softly on the bit, he is in fact talking with us. This is proof that the horse has relaxed his top line, and is in a state of mental and emotional comfort. Relaxation of the lower jaw allows Deglutition. When the horse relaxes his lower jaw, he "deglutates." This means he lifts the bit with his tongue and his salivary glands are activated.

The tongue is a very important factor as it is related and connected to the activation of the core.

In humans when you practice more sophisticated yoga asanas or postures, you need to position your tongue on the top of your palate.

When the horse achieves this state, meaning relaxation of the lower jaw and the lifting of his tongue we are able to have the horse in deglutition. He is able to lightly chew on the bit as mentioned in the F. E. I. rules for the halt.

We are able to keep him in that state, the mental and emotional relaxation he is close to perfect. That is the moment in which we can experience oneness.

Conversely, the opposite is a clenched jaw that we see so often in horses that are tensed and locked in place. This relaxation is impossible when we have forced our horses' mouth and jaw shut with devices such as Crank nose bands and with forced pulling contact, especially with German or draw reins. The rigidity of the back does not allow for the soft mouth.

Please refer to Thomas Myers, Article in Massage Magazine December 2018

TO DOMINIQUE: How can we know what is truly in the best interest of our horse?

Ask yourself if you were a horse, how would you like to be treated. If you come from this place you can always judge what is best for your horse.

TO DOMINIQUE: You have practiced French Classical Dressage all your life. But you have gone beyond the classical principles and teach people about the mental communication with horses. When and how did you learn about this unusual approach?

When I was very young, I used to experiment with my imagination, my breathing and what became visualization. My intuition led me to apply the technique to the horses. I discovered that horses read your mind. They do not anticipate, as so many believe. That is when I developed the "two minds" thinking. One that the horse (or anybody) could read, and the other one that I locate in the back of my mind. Nobody could access that picture, until I brought it forward. It has worked for me with thousands of horses. It was so effective that I wanted to teach people about it, so they could use this visualization skill as well.

Secondly, I always felt in my heart, the horse connection with God, or any supreme presence, whatever name you are comfortable with. I always thought horses were in our life for a higher purpose. I always felt those moments of oneness were very highly spiritual. A few years ago, I came up with a formula "lightness for enlightenment."

They are in our life to help us become our higher self.

You can understand now, how horrified I feel with what I am witnessing in this "modern competition" world.

It is why we need to defend them in order for them to accomplish their mission.

On the practical level, our responsibility is to make them comfortable and happy. That is why, for me, Shoulder-In is so important because it is a movement that is the epitome of translating the pure nature of the relationship we aspire to. Only when the horse is physically, mentally and emotionally comfortable that he is able to show you how he would like to perform the movement, in order to meet brilliance.

Then it is our part to practice with self-discipline the *Descente de Main, Descente de Jambes,* in a very simple movement that will trigger a change of consciousness.

TO DOMINIQUE: WHAT do you mean by "change of consciousness"?

Change of consciousness is simply a different way to look at and feel about things. Suddenly, most of the equestrian "problems" and questions disappear. It is also true, in life in general.

This is happening when I teach my golden ball meditation. If you are interested in this read about the life of St. Germain

This way of thinking is available to anybody of any age and any skill level with horses. Generally, children are already there. And the horses are ALWAYS there, waiting for us.

Greta Thunberg, the sixteen-year-old inspirational climate activist from Sweden said in a recent speech:

> *"You lied to us. You gave us false hope. You told us that the future was something to look forward to"...."I want you to feel the fear I feel every day and then I want you to act. I want you to act as you would in a crisis. I want you to act as if your house is on fire."*

This incredibly powerful statement about the state of our environment brings to mind the same urgency we face for our horses.

This is an excellent time to make the point also, that we are advocating not only for "Dressage" horses.

ALL horses, be they Racing, Western show, Driving, Polo, and including the horse in our back yard, need and deserve to be treated with love and grace. When we are ignorant it is easy to be abusive. Education, understanding, and compassion should be the rule of the day.

CONCLUSION

Liz and I acknowledge that there are numerous repetitions throughout this book. We feel they are all needed. It was not an easy task, and, like most of you, we love horses and every day we try to honor them as much as we are able to.

We also love the art of riding, which is a sublimation of the unique relationship we have with horses. With that said, we do not enjoy the present situation.

What to do?

First, for yourself as much as possible, we should have the necessary tools to understand them better. As you partner with your horse, ask how can we interest them better in the dance? How can we make the dance easier, more interesting, vibrant and joyful?

Share your passion with your friends, both two legged and four legged.

For the big picture, if you feel you can, be an advocate, do not be silent.

Make yourself heard. Make sure that people know there is a soft and gentle way to train horses, to be with them.

Be their voice. Horses are part of the world. Like the climate, like the environment, like the whole planet, horses need our voices.

Our best hope is to give the tools to young people as well as everyone, in order to provide more choices, more inspiration and to discover the never-ending search for oneness, one earth.

With Love,
Dominique

We are available for answering questions. See our contact information at the end of the book.

*Dressage should protect the horse, allowing for all the beauty and knowledge they possess.
Photo by Rebekah McNeff, Horse is Japu DB*

> "Seeing, one could say that the whole of life lies in the word SEEING."
> —Teilhard de Chardin.

After reading all of this,

Enjoy your horse.

If you want to compete by all means do so. But please do not compromise your relationship with your beloved horse and do not betray him in the quest for a ribbon.

If you go to the show and you see abuse, please speak up. Report to the steward.

Pick judges carefully, use showing as a learning experience.

Write letters to national magazines. They may not publish them now but they will take notice of repeated comments.

What future will horses have in Dressage? It is up to us. Photo by Davi Carrano

> *"Do not be with him, be him with joy."*
> *"NO difference no separation."*
> *"Lightness is the essence of your union, Body Mind and Soul."*
> —Dominique Barbier

> "Lightness is to allow your horse to be himself, giving, loving, breathing with him, expressing himself."
>
> "Lightness will give you the feeling of enlightenment."
>
> —Dominique Barbier

BROKEN OR BEAUTIFUL

109

APPENDIX

As Dominique and I were doing our research for this book I came upon a copy of this article in my library. It was startling to realize that 44 years ago we were already seeing unhappy horses in International competition.

I was fortunate enough to attend those Olympic games as well. At the time I was very new to Dressage and had seen very few Grand Prix horses. I anticipated seeing horses dancing with riders in total harmony. But I recall going home and feeling a bit of disappointment that the beauty and magic I had anticipated that were not there.

The biggest difference between the scene then and now is the added abuse of horses. We had not seen the advent of Rollkur nor L. D. R. at that time. Very few rode horses over-bent as it was understood that this was wrong.

Ironically, this article is just as apropos today as the day it was written. The day has come to decide if we will be back again to ask the same questions 40 more years from now.

—Liz

Donald Weinberg, Editor of Dressage and CT Magazine, Interviewed Dominique for the article below. They had met at Talland School of Equitation in Cirenchester, England in 1972, and became great friends. A few years later when Dominique moved to Sun Valley Idaho, Donald joined him to continue his riding education.

The article was published in the March 1977 Edition of *Dressage & CT* Magazine is included here in its entirety.

This is the first in a series of conversations with young, professional dressage trainers in America. With the many established professionals in the country to choose from, we found ourselves in a quandary over whom to pick first. Our solution was to begin the series with a relatively unknown professional who has just immigrated to the United States, Dominique Barbier.

Dominique Barbier grew up in Poitiers, a town in France not far from Saumur. He started riding as a youth on weekends and after school. His first regular riding "job" was for a man who imported green Irish hunters to France. He would put young Dominique on one of the new arrivals, close the doors to the arena, and come back twenty minutes later. If Dominique were still on, well and good; if not, a torrent of invective was rained on him. It was an effective if not conventional way to develop a secure seat.

Dominique's first more orthodox studies were with John Lasseter, B. H. S. I., and Brian Young, F. B. H. S., at Crabbett Park in England, where he received his B. H. S. A. I. in 1967. He then went back to France to get the equivalent French qualification, the moniteur, in 1968, and also to take a short course for young professionals at Saumur. For the next year and a half, he traveled through France (and occasionally to Germany) learning the horse business in the method of compagnons, or what we would call short apprenticeships, working at race stables, three-day stables, hunt stables, learning all the phases of equine endeavor.

He spent 1970 in the Veterinary and Biological Service of the French Army training remounts, and then continued his equestrian education back in England at the Talland School of Equitation, where he was both student and instructor. He received his B. H. S. I. there in 1972. At Talland, Dominique had a lot of experience with three-day eventing and also worked with Mrs. Charles Sivewright, F. B. H. S., D. B. H. S., whose primary interest is dressage and who has made several Grand Prix horses. Then, from 1973 through 1975, he studied with Nuno Oliveira in Portugal and started the training of his two horses, Dom Pasquale and Dom Giovani.

Dominique now lives in Illinois and is associated with Dressage Centre Ltd. in Chicago Heights.

What is your approach to training? When you're training a horse, what are you trying to produce? What are your goals? Have you a method?

Before I start to answer any technical questions, I want to make sure that you understand that my approach is very different from other professionals' or any approach that has ever been done. My background is the classical school, the French Classical school, when dressage was an art, and I feel that I in a very small way have a different approach to it, in that most of my emphasis is on the mind, and that's never been done before. The ability to communicate with another being with your brain, a lot of people think about it, but it's never been done as a direct approach to training of the horse and training of the rider. What I say here is not the same thing said differently, it's a completely different concept of approaching life and approaching your horse. My whole idea in life, my whole goal in life is to try to train my horse and have my horse happy, and be able to give the people the same feeling that I have towards my horses.

Now, the first thing to establish is that we are all looking for perfection, okay? Perfection is riding with your mind, that is very, very important, with your mind, with your seat, with very little leg, light leg (We have the French expression, "The leg must breath with the horse"), and no hands, the contact just the weight of the reins: that is perfection. And when I say the horse is light, of course I don't mean light to start with. I mean the horse must be first relaxed, then on the bit, and then he must become both active and light.

Now, when I think about my goal in training horses, I think first of all you must establish a mental relationship with your horse. That means he has to know what you expect him to do, as simple as it might be, and you must know that you are going to have it, without force, with a calm determination. Training of horses is to have a good understanding of their mental and physical difficulties and to try to ease those difficulties. To a very high degree it's psychology of the horses, knowing what horses need, and just helping them through the movement you ask for.

Something you have to remember all the time is that the horse is performing, you are not. You prepare the horse, build the impulsion, you position the horse, you ask for the movement, and he must produce it. That can be as simple as going from the halt to the walk or a turn to the right. What we must realize is that ninety-something percent is straight mental.

Now, of course, if we are thinking about such refined aids, we have to put the horse in the condition that he is able to understand them. If your position is not good, if you don't have a good understanding of the length of the rein and the correct over-all position, you are not going to be able to communicate brain to brain. But if you are correct in your body and especially in your mind, that means complete relaxation of the whole body, then you are able to make the horse realize exactly what you want, and I think that can be done by everybody, and done every day without force, and the horse is happy and moving as if he were free. That's the name of the game, letting the horse move. A lot of people want to train their horses, but they themselves create their own problems. First of all, you must sit on the horse without upsetting him, then try to help him; that is called training. But most people have not achieved the first step, they still upset the horse.

How do you teach people to do this? As you said, you not only train horses yourself, you want to teach others to train horses in this way. Is it not difficult?

No, actually it's very simple. We are very lucky in this profession in that most of the riders are women, and women are very sensitive individuals, most of them. And what is very important to me, most of them are very small, refined, and light. They don't have great strength, and thus you must find an approach that is going to allow them to work with the horse and dominate that tremendous power without any fight, because they simply cannot physically overpower the horse.

Everybody has the feel through their fingers and through their brain, the only thing they must do is use their brain and try to understand what they are feeling. And that can be done every day under good instruction. The people can develop their feel, and by developing their feel work with their horses without any force.

For example, a lot of my teaching, clinic teaching, is putting the horse on the bit without any effort, and that is no effort, any horse.

When you say putting the horse on the bit with no effort, you mean no force, no physical effort, do you not? Obviously, one must make an effort.

Yes, certainly, but mental. You have to put the horse in a certain situation, mental and physical, that he is able to be on the bit and he understands it, and he likes it better on the bit. The horse on the bit is a horse who is happy, because he is able to balance himself. Now, there is a lot of misunderstanding about being on the bit. The horse on the bit is with you 100%, mentally and physically, and the horse can be on the bit in a long frame, not only in collection.

Looking at your own learning experience, you studied with Nuno Oliveira in Portugal. Now, he's been around a long time, and he has often been accused of being circus. By association, then, if his kind of riding is circus, then the same people will accuse you of being circus.

Now, I love a good circus. I don't know why to supposedly classical dressage riders circus is a bad word. They don't know, perhaps, enough about what dressage was, that all the top *ecuyers*, all the people whose books they read, went in the circus and actually performed in the circus, because at that time the people had a certain appreciation of beauty and also in the last century, the circus was the only place dressage was displayed.

Of course, you have a bad aspect of circus, as you have a bad aspect of dressage, that is very showy, and the routine of showing is unnatural and bad. But I would like the people who criticize the circus people, the good circus people, to try to be circus because you cannot do what he can do.

I have the greatest respect for *Mestre* Nuno Oliveira, because he has trained so many horses to the highest level that he cannot count them anymore, there are too many. And that man has such respect for his art that he does not bother answering the accusations, because he **knows**; I believe nobody knows half of what he knows. He is a very gifted individual and has done a lot of work, nobody can know how much work he has and does put into it.

And that is the answer of training, its work. You can be gifted, but if you don't work, you go nowhere. And as far as being accused of circus, when the horse is light, you drop the rein. What is a better feeling than to have the horse performing passage or piaffe or high collection movements or levade with a loop in the rein, what is a better feeling? And it is possible, I see it, I do it every day, and I make my people do it so they can feel that riding is not driving on a retaining hand, restraining hands. Collection is not compression; no force is involved.

How do you regard competition, its uses, its purposes, its consequences?

I think competition is very good. Competition can be a great help to many people, especially when they get interested in competition. Now, I would like to see the people compete with their horses, not against their horses. By that I mean that the person who goes showing should have a good time and want the horse to have a good time, to have a happy horse, and not care so much about a number of points. For me, the art of riding is not a number of points. If my horse enjoys it, if I think he has been correct, that's my pleasure. For a lot of people, competition is very serious business that has nothing to do with the love of their animal, and I think that is very, very, very bad.

The primary interest is trying to have the horse trained and happy. The horse must be happy, the rider must be happy. We compete to know where we stand compared to other people, if we are interested in it. For example, I am not. I am the least competitive person in the world, but I do agree that some people are competitive and I help them in that matter. But I want competition to serve the horse, that the horse would be better afterwards.

Going from that, then, what do you think of competition standards as they are today, and F. E. I. and AHSA tests, what they call for and the way they are judged?

It's a very difficult question to answer. I am very disappointed in the standards in international competition, not mentioning the lower levels. To my knowledge, right now in America we have better lower standards, better lower tests, as far as quality than at international levels.

International level standards I think are a disaster. Why? Because, and I am not the only one thinking this, we think that riding is an art, and any method that goes against the horse, that makes people try to reduce their horses to machines and try to desensitize them, is wrong, is against dressage.

Dressage is to make your horse more sensitive and more educated; you ask him to do a movement and the horse gives you the movement. Without artistic beauty in a performance, it's not dressage. That's why to my mind, we have to make a big distinction between what classical dressage is and what they have made competition dressage become.

They being the F. E. I.?
No, not really the F. E. I., I think the F. E. I. is a consequence of what competition has become now. They are obliged to adapt their rules to what they see, and because what they see right now, and I am very sorry about it, it is not at all beautiful, it's very limited, it's very hard. You have a feeling of so much force and so much brutality, and no pleasure, it's a very sad story. You see people sad-faced, you see horses sad; they don't enjoy themselves.

Is that what you saw at the Olympics? You were there? What were your reactions?
Yes, I was there. At the Olympics, my reaction was a little stronger than that. I think that, without going into details, most of the movements were not correct. I would have been happy to see the gold medalist win with thirty-five percent. I'll just take one example, there was one pirouette to the left by Klimke that was the only correct pirouette; all the others were between zero and three, because they were all four-beat canter. Now, four-beat canter is the worst thing you can have. It's absolutely incorrect

What is very sad is that I am not sure if the perfect horse had come into the ring at the Olympics the judges would have recognized it. By perfect horse, I mean. . . you have a little word that is a very big totem in modern riding, lightness. Everybody talks about it, but we never see it. Light is the horse with the contact, and the contact is the weight of the rein. That is lightness. We cannot have the horse "sort of" light or light some of the time. We have him either light or not light, no compromise. And right now, we have people riding with fifty pounds in each hand as a regular thing. To such a degree that now top instructors go around the country teaching that if you have not fifty pounds in each hand, you cannot train a horse. That is the most absurd thing I have ever heard.

What happens, then, to your students, who are riding in lightness, where they go into a test, and they get their test back with fours and fives and the comment, "No contact"?
I think the judges must be a little more educated in what they are doing. Of course, what is very important, the loop in the rein is fantastic if the horse is on the bit and is active. I don't think about the loop in the rein with the horse upside down, I'm speaking about the horse absolutely round, in a very correct frame, and active. Most people misunderstand the concept of the loop in the rein. They

say the horse is behind a bit. This is an incorrect expression. What matters is if the horse is behind or in front of your leg and he must be in front of your leg.

Now for the people who come back with test that's a no contact, first of all I try to educate the judges and try to make them feel a little better about lightness; if the horse is active and is correct with a loop in the rein it's very close to perfection, and they have to know about that perfection. I hope we will get to many people that way, because it's surely more enjoyable

If we don't we can have a visual sophistication of the whole thing, and ride the test for the same light contact but with a straight rein, which is a pity, because I think that nobody who is able to ride that way is not tempted to give the rein to the horse. The same way that I think every gift a trainer is tempted to do all that people call circus movements. I don't know anybody who is able, for example, to canter on the spot (that's why I am trying to do with one of my horses right now, who will be able to do it in a perfect, three beat canter I don't know anybody else who is able to do it and does not do it!

In other words, the temptation to see what one can do is irresistible

Yes, exactly, if it is correct, and I insist on that, because I am the first to fight bad circus or bad dressage, things that are not correct. My background is the French classical school, and I stick to that, and I want my horses to be very correct. My canter on the spot will be three- beat canter, I will never do it in four-beat canter. The same horse is able now to do three pirouettes in a row and perfect three- beat canter. We can take movies to see the sequence of the legs. And I'm glad that so many people have taken movies of the Olympics, because they would be able to see the difference.

For better or for worse, many people are interested in what you've done, what you have accomplished, usually expressed in what you have won, what teams have you made. So, as a trainer, what have you accomplished so far?

First of all, I am very young, therefore it's a question of time. Now, I Have trained my two horses, Pasquale and Giovanni, to as high of level as possible. They are my first complete horses.

I am very pleased to say that I do not count anymore, from during my life in Europe and the four years of clinics in this country, the number of horses I put in flying changes, flying changes in sequences, and a little passage a little piaffe; a little of everything that you can start in a clinic situation where the people can take advantage and learn and feel from it.

Now, something else that is very important, training of the horses to make the horse more enjoyable to ride, that's the whole reason we are writing. And I do not consider piaffe or passage or flying changes as movements, ends in themselves; I consider them helps, it means to make the horse better. That's why we start those movements very early, too early for the so-called very, very classical dressage riders who say you must not do it so early.

Too early, what do you mean by that?

Meaning that if you consider starting your piaffe before your horse is six or seven or eight, they really consider you a bad person, that you are something that is too much. And I never ask too much from any of my horses, they are all the time being understanding and giving me the movement.

But I am using the beginning of the piaffe, what we called the mobilization of the haunches, just as a suppling exercise, to get more activity; sometimes we use passage for rhythm, sometimes we use flying changes for general suppleness and unlocking the back. We use those movements to make the horse better. My goal is not to have my horse in piaffe or in passage, it's to have my horse better, that I can feel every day I do less, and he is better.

I use all the movements, all or any of the movements at a given time, for a purpose. My horse might do them all at three or four during his training, but what takes time is the refinement, the perfection of the movements. Piaffe or passage will never be new things to my horses, a new surprise for them to learn when they are seven or eight. When I start a young horse and piaffe, it is then just, as I said, a mobilization of the haunches, but I know I will ultimately have a finished, correct piaffe. Its development is a continuing, perfecting progression, and I have that progression in my mind from the start.

And I want to add something here, we were talking about competition. In competition you must produce specified movements in a set order. Now it's fairly easy to make a horse lengthen and piaffe and passage and pirouette and everything. When we start to put all these movements together to make a Grand Prix, I know it's a different story. Now, I do not accept mediocrity because we have to put the movements together. That's why it's very difficult to judge a Grand Prix test or perform a Grand Prix test; I do not want to sacrifice the beautiful feeling and the beauty of the movements because we have to put them together in a rigid, prescribed sequence.

Okay, but at the same time, you've said you think competition is a good thing, it can help people, so the only way, not the only way, one can have a Kuer[1] classes, but other than that, in order to judge ten horses, you will have to have a test with prescribed movements. Do you think it's impossible, really, to train a horse to be able, when you ask, to produce a series of movements in a particular order? Can that not be done without mechanizing the horse? Is the only way to do it to sacrifice?

---

1   Musical freestyle. ~Editor's note.

Yes, I think that right now the way the judges do their job and the way the pressure is put on the people, the only way is to mechanize the horse. And I am not interested in and refuse to do that.

What then is the alternative for comparison on an international level? What would you have done?

We can do as they do and some other sports, and I know that I am not the first person to suggest this. We have in ice skating compulsory figures and we have a freestyle. I think that past a certain level a free-style ride would allow us much more to express beauty than just a test to go over and over again, and I am sure that if the rider fell off, the horse would still do it, because he does it for six years in a row, and he knows it by heart. Of course, that's not true, that's just a manner of speaking, but that's the feeling you get when you watch. The judge must be looking for a good, a beautiful performance. My ideal is that somebody who knows nothing about the art would sit there and say, "God, that is beautiful, it's such a beautiful thing." Now, I am sorry to say that when I was at the Olympics, I was very sad, there was very little beauty, very little, very little. The people and the horses were very sad, very unhappy, all of them, and I think part of it is because their relationship with the horse is absolutely wrong. We cannot treat them like machines.

Of course, if you try to mechanize the horses and if you like it, it's good; if the people who do the competition the way it is now enjoy it, I say to those people just carry-on, do it, but you have nothing to do with me. I love my horses and I want to have a companionship; I want what everybody, I think at the start before they become competition riders, especially at the high levels, wants. They love their horses, they want to perform together with their horses, and not be brutal and hard and have to force them.

How do the writings of the past masters, and which ones, influence your training, your methods and theories?

What is important is that I try to redo what the old French classical school did. The perfection in the French classical school was to be able to ride the horse in what we call *descente de main, descente de jambe*, which means no hands and no legs, the horse performing all on its own.

All de la Guérinière influences me a lot. And what I try to see through the old masters is who would be able to give me an answer with the modern horse, the horses we ride today, who are pretty different from those they had at that time. The closest we have now is, of course, the Lusitanian. [The Lusitanian, bred in Portugal for hundreds of years, is similar to the Spanish horse, the Andalusian.] But when you ride Thoroughbreds, it's an entirely different thing, a man who is a great help, and who is very difficult man to understand (which is why he was condemned by many) is Baucher.

So, de la Guérinière and then Baucher, Baucher and his followers, who influenced me through the modern horse like the Thoroughbred. But I do not follow anyone man, Baucher or anyone else. What I do is make a synthesis of their ideas plus my own experience.

When you read a book, you have to take what corresponds to your personality and what you are looking for, and not read a book as you read a cooking recipe. No system, no method, just very big principles, and I use a big principle of the French school. Everything must be correct, light, active, easy. If it's not easy, it's wrong. Now that is a big principle, but as far as training a horse, I have absolutely no method. How can you have a set method when you were dealing with individuals?

What do you think of training devices such as Draw reins, Chambons, and so on?

I think they are the best and the worst thing. I do not recommend that anybody use them, but with people who know them, and they are very rare, they can be very good.

I myself use hardly anything except side reins on the longe to put the horse in the proper shape to start with. I am against longeing a horse in the wrong shape, that's the worst thing, too. Once again, with side reins, you have to know what to do with them and how to adjust them.

Of course, all those pieces of equipment, Chambons and Gogues, all that is French. We try to invent new tricks, but that's bad, I would not advise it. I did use a lot of them early in my life for special reasons, and actually I got very good results, but I don't like them or want anybody to use them.

You work a lot on the longe, usually before you get on.

Yes, before a ride. You have two things, you have longeing for work, when you want to produce something on the longe; and you have longeing just to warm up your horse, just to make him loose to warm him up in the right frame without your mistake on the top. That's what I do most of the time. It's like you when you get out of bed and you are a little bit stiff, if somebody sat on you to start with, you would be in bad shape, but given time to warm up a bit, then why not? But you cannot expect a horse who is a little bit stiff, not warm, to have you directly sit on him and work.

First, I longe them, and then I work in-hand. Now, work in-hand is very, very, very important. I think it is something that most of the trainers don't know about, it's a lost art. Work in-hand is a great, great help because you can see what you are doing, you can see the improvement in the horses, you can see their mental and physical state, and you further warm them up on both sides without weight on top.

Work in-hand is very difficult, it's an art, you must practice a lot. I teach my students how to do it because it's very important to know where the problem is and try to solve it later on. When you work [the horse] in-hand and you see the horse, you see his eye, and you are able to spot much more easily where the problem is, mental or physical, and then try to find a solution.

As far as seeing the difficulty, which side it is on, a lot of people try to get help from books, and as everybody knows, books help the people who know, not the people who don't know, I'm afraid. And they tell you that a horse must be absolutely straight, straight meaning even on both sides. That is absolutely ridiculous. The horse has been twisted for a number of months in his mother, and they get out of the way we get out, just absolutely crooked. What we can have as a horse straight optically speaking. But, in fact, as far as feeling, it's not at all the same. We never have naturally, for example, the same degree of shoulder-in to the right and to the left. It's not at all possible naturally because they are naturally crooked. What we try to do is to have the horse straight in his head, straight mentally, and then we can produce apparently identical shoulder-ins on both sides. His mental state allows him to look even. But as far as straight physically, we have to compensate as we ride or school, because each horse has his own difficulties.

Do you prefer to train a horse from scratch, starting with a green horse, or would you rather a fourth level horse with potential to go from there?
I prefer a young horse.

You mentioned the Lusitanian horse being closest to the classical horses, and you have Lusitanians yourself. For training, do you prefer any particular breed?
No, I think there is no breed, that is one of the big mistakes now, that people try to breed horses with the wrong goals in mind, thinking they are breeding for dressage. I think it's absolutely ridiculous to breed a horse down, to bring the horse down to man's low standard now, to make him able to produce as a machine. I think it's wrong.

I like any horse with good conformation who has some spirit in him, who is a good athlete, and you can find a good athlete in any breed. For example, you find super purebred Arabs were very good for classical dressage. You find some Trakehners, you find some in any breed. Any horse who is a good athlete is good for classical dressage. The horse I would dream to have in dressage would be Secretariat. That means when you have a good athlete, he is good for everything, and I reject the idea of breeding a horse to try to put his brain to a certain level of what I would call low-standard dressage.

Why did you come to the United States?

That's a very good question. First of all, I think that I am the type of person who has been American all his life. By that I mean I'm a person who is going forward all the time.

But I came here basically because I think that you have in this country very deep interest for what you are doing, and when you were interested and are able to give the people what they want, I think that they love you, and when they have something to give them, they are open minded enough that they are able to, the word is bad, but to take advantage of you.

In Europe, we are a little bit too traditional. If you can ride, if you're not old, you don't know anything. That's the bad side of tradition. On the other hand, Americans have a lot of complexes, they say, "Oh, you are European, your country is doing that and that in that, you are the greatest." I think that's not true; I think there's more interest in America for dressage than you have in all Europe.

More than in Germany, where you have a CDI or other big show almost every weekend, where they will fill Grand Prix classes with ninety horses, Prix St. George's classes with 125 horses? Do you really think there's more interest in the United States?

I think there is more of my kind of interest in America, more freedom. Who enjoyed regimentation? Once again, I don't want any sort of political or ethnic fight about it, but it's just the fact that you have many ways to dance. And I prefer a French or Italian minuet to Bavarian waltz.

Everything that's regimental I don't like, and I am not sure Americans like it either. They have free minds, they have horses different from over there, and they ride for different purposes. You ride the way you are, and it's a mistake to try to be a German in the brain and to try to make a Holsteiner out of your American Thoroughbred, who is one of the nicest breeds for dressage that you have.

Then the American should stick with their Thoroughbreds rather than importing and breeding Trakehners or Hanoverians or other warmbloods? There's nothing wrong with Thoroughbred for dressage? You'll hear very often that the Thoroughbred is very beautiful, he is an athlete, but his mind has been destroyed by breeding for speed, that they are, by and large, crazy, all they want to do is run. You don't think so?

No. You were speaking about the brain of the horses destroyed. I'm afraid I will speak about the brain of the people destroyed. But if they are open minded, if they are riders, then they know better. Now a rider is somebody different, a rider is not somebody who just sits on the horse. A rider is a different person. That's what we have lost through the years. He's a person who every day, every single second of his life asks himself questions. He's not somebody who stays where he is, he's all the time looking for something.

And what better than a Thoroughbred to make you look for something? I know it's frustrating, a lot of people can't take that, that's why they have what I would call those special breeds, who are for people who don't want that challenge. But I would like those people to do car racing.

We are dealing with an animal, and dealing with an animal is dealing with a person. I like to have clever friends, I like to be around good people and clever friends; I'd like to be around clever horses, I like the horse whom I teach something today and tomorrow he's going to try to use the same thing against me. So, who is more clever, he or I? I am sorry, but most horses are much more clever than people. That's where the trouble is.

And instead of, as I have said, trying to breed the horses down, to take away their cleverness, their spirit, we have to sensitize them, and the Thoroughbred is one of the best horses for doing that. And especially your American Thoroughbred by his conformation. It's a good conformation for dressage. I have three horses in training who are Thoroughbred, and I think we are going to see them in competition soon, not that I like it that way, but it's the only way to have the people see, and they are going to see that high collection movements are very possible for Thoroughbreds.

Now, you cannot ride a Thoroughbred as you ride an Arab or as you ride a half-bred horse, you have to ride differently. And why people don't like them for dressage is because their concepts of riding are wrong, and they try to force the horses, to compress the horses. You cannot force a Thoroughbred, you have to deal with him, you must not force.

Staying with breeds for a minute, it's said of Lusitanian's, Spanish horses, that are nice horses, but can't extend. Do you agree with that?

No, I don't agree. Once again, we cannot generalize by breed. You have some thoroughbreds who cannot extend either. Therefore, it's not a question of that. The Lusitanian has been bred for many years for very special purposes. They were fighting horses, bull fighting or war fighting, or for working with cattle, and dressage at beginning started with that.

Everything in classical dressage, in the old school, was collection. The extension is the concept of modern dressage, which is something new, coming with the Thoroughbred. It's true that the Lusitano has a certain ability to sit more than other horses, and by that I mean to collect themselves more in lightness. But they can extend, too. Two of mine have very decent, correct extensions.

How do you view your profession and other professionals?

I have a great respect for my profession in my art. I try to be an *Ecuyer*, and being an *Ecuyer* is something very special, not just a profession but a way of living, it's a way of being. I wish more people would have the same view of their job. [*Maitre Ecuyer* was the title of the Master of Horse for the French kings. In the current Petit Larousse, *Ecuyer* is defined as "professor of equitation." The word implies not only consummate skill in training horses, but also the ability to transmit one's art.

There's been talk about certification and licensing at professionals in this country, very much as is done in many European countries. What do you think about that?

I think it's a very good idea. You have too many trainers, or supposedly trainers, who go around the country and start teaching, but actually they don't know. You cannot just go to a university and teach medicine, so why should you be able to just say, "I am a trainer, and start teaching? I am looking forward to it, but once again, like every certification, every restriction, it has to be done well.

Going back to the beginning, why did you choose to concentrate on dressage, having looked at and experienced it all?

I went through indoor show jumping, stadium jumping, cross country, three-day eventing, hunting; I had a tremendous time, it's a great sport. The best thing that I would say to dressage people is please jump before you go into dressage. It gives you the feeling of forward movement, a thing we rarely see in dressage horses. They must go forward, you must have the same feeling riding a piaffe and jumping a seven-foot wall, basically speaking.

I think that in eventing, part of your pleasure is more physical. By that I mean it's a great thing to canter around the country, and jumping generally is one of the more marvelous things I've ever done, but at the same time, once you have done it, you have done it; for me it's very limited. In dressage you have a so much greater possibility for true, deep relation with your horse than any other disciplines

The way I'm approaching the training of my horse, that means the French school plus a very important emphasis of the mind, I work with the horse's true personality, and when you change horses to reveal their true personality, it's like changing the world. Jumping over fences is pretty much the same thing all the way around, except that's not true, because you have a different way of jumping every horse, too. But dressage corresponds more to my sort of mind, going deeper into everything, and especially changing horses. For each one you have a completely different approach.

We know how difficult it is to have people in the army or to try to make them into numbers, and that's what many people try to do with horses. I am against that completely, I want the horses coming to me when they are ready to work, as I do with Pasquale; I turn him loose, and then he comes to me when he is ready, when he wants to work. And when they do that, you expect them to give you everything, and they do.

The best hunters and the best jumpers use dressage in their training, they call it flatwork. Can a high-level dressage horse benefit from jumping? Would you ever jump your horses?

Yes, I do jump horses, especially at the very beginning. I think what a lot of people call dressage before Fourth Level is not dressage, it's just flat work, it's good riding or bad riding, but it's flat work, communicating to the horse the basics. I believe that a horse must be Third Level before he does anything else, and that can be jumping, hunting, polo. It's part of the basic training. When you start to go higher than that in dressage, with my kind of thinking you had better stick to what you are doing.

Now, that doesn't say that you cannot take your horse over a fence whenever you want, because he is a horse, and I all the time jump my horses, whatever level they are.

For example, with the Pasquale, if you're out on a hack, you would jump him?

Sure, and actually, that would do a lot of good for his own sanity.

So, you will jump your most highly schooled horses as a mental release, whereas at the lower level the jumping is to teach them something.

Yes, yes. On the same line, it's very bad to work the horses indoors all the time. I work them outside, and I turn them loose as much as I can.

Loose meaning in the arena?

Yes, in the arena or outside if I can afford it. Too much work makes a horse sour, you have to know the day when you do not work him and you hack him, asking nothing. If that particular day you work, that would be wrong and bad, therefore don't do it, go on a hack. Also, you can hack and have a little working station somewhere in the field and then come back. It's very good for their mental side. You must make the horse like his job. If he doesn't like it, he's not going to give his heart, it's like for anything.

Just in closing, I know that some of what I will say will be controversial, and I will be perfectly willing to elaborate on or discuss anything with anybody on a constructive basis.

Ultraje VO ridden by Dominique Barbier Photo by Candida von Braun

BIBLIOGRAPHY

Reflections on Equestrian Art, by Nuno Oliveira translated by Phyllis Field, J. A. Allen & Company Limited 1976

The Alchemy of Lightness, by Dominique Barbier & Dr. Maria Katsamanis, Trafalgar Square Books 2013

Dressage in the French Tradition, by Dom Diogo de Bragança, Xenophon Press 2011

Dressage for the New Age, Dominique Barbier, Prentice Hall Press 1990

XENOPHON PRESS LIBRARY

www.XenophonPress.com
Xenophon Press is dedicated to the preservation
of classical equestrian literature.
We bring both new and old works to English-speaking riders.

30 Years with Master Nuno Oliveira, Henriquet 2011
A Rider's Survival from Tyranny, de Kunffy 2012
Another Horsemanship, Racinet 1994
Austrian Art of Riding, Poscharnigg 2015
Broken or Beautiful: The Struggle of Modern Dressage, Barbier 2021
Classic Show Jumping: the de Nemethy Method, de Nemethy 2016
Divide and Conquer Book 1, Lemaire de Ruffieu 2016
Divide and Conquer Book 2, Lemaire de Ruffieu 2017
Dressage for the 21st Century, Belasik 2001
Dressage in the French Tradition, Diogo de Bragança 2011
Dressage Principles and Techniques: A Blueprint for the Serious Rider, Tavora 2018
Dressage Principles Illuminated, Expanded Edition, de Kunffy 2021
Dressage Sabbatical: A Year of Riding with Classical Master Paul Belasik, Caslar 2016
École de Cavalerie Part II, Robichon de la Guérinière 1992, 2015
Equine Osteopathy: What the Horses Have Told Me, Giniaux 2014
Fragments from the Writings of Max Ritter von Weyrother, Fane 2017
François Baucher: The Man and His Method, Baucher/Nelson 2013
General Chamberlin: America's Equestrian Genius, Matha 2020
Great Horsewomen of the 19th Century in the Circus, Nelson 2015
Gymnastic Exercises for Horses Volume II, Eleanor Russell 2013
H. Dv. 12 German Cavalry Manual of Horsemanship, Reinhold 2014
Handbook of Jumping Essentials, Lemaire de Ruffieu 2015
Handbook of Riding Essentials, Lemaire de Ruffieu 2015
Healing Hands, Giniaux, DVM 1998

Horse Training: Outdoors and High School, Beudant 2014
Horsemanship and Horsemastership Volume 1, U.S. Cavalry School, 2021
I, Siglavy, Asay 2018
Learning to Ride, Santini 2016
Legacy of Master Nuno Oliveira, Millham 2013
Lessons in Lightness: Expanded Edition, Mark Russell 2019
Methodical Dressage of the Riding Horse, Faverot de Kerbrech 2010
Military Equitation or, A Method of Breaking Horses, and Teaching Soldiers to Ride, Pembroke, *and A Treatise on Military Equitation,* Tyndale 2018
Principles of Dressage and Equitation, a.k.a. Breaking and Riding, Fillis 2017
Racinet Explains Baucher, Racinet 1997
Relaxing the Neck, Mouth and Jaw: more Lessons in Lightness DVD, Russell, 2021
Riding and Schooling Horses, Chamberlin 2020
Riding by Torchlight, Cord 2019
Riding in Rhyme, Davies, 2021
Science and Art of Riding in Lightness, Stodulka 2015
The Art of Riding a Horse, D'Eisenberg 2015
The Art of Traditional Dressage, Volume I DVD, de Kunffy 2013
The Chamberlin Reader, Chamberlin/Matha, 2020
The de Nemethy Method: A training seminar, 8 DVD set, de Nemethy 2019
The Ethics and Passions of Dressage Expanded Edition, de Kunffy 2013
The Forward Impulse, Santini 2016
The Gymnasium of the Horse, Steinbrecht 2018
The Horses, a novel, Elaine Walker 2015
The Italian Tradition of Equestrian Art, Tomassini 2014
The Maneige Royal, de Pluvinel 2010, 2015
The New Method of Dressing Horses, Cavendish 2020
The Portuguese School of Equestrian Art, de Oliveira/da Costa 2012
The Spanish Riding School & Piaffe and Passage, Decarpentry 2013
To Amaze the People with Pleasure and Delight, Walker 2015
Total Horsemanship, Racinet 1999
Training Hunters, Jumpers, and Hacks, Chamberlin 2019
Training with Master Nuno Oliveira, 2 DVD set, Eleanor Russell 2016
Truth in the Teaching of Master Nuno Oliveira, Eleanor Russell 2015
Wisdom of Master Nuno Oliveira, de Coux 2012

www.ingramcontent.com/pod-product-compliance
Lightning Source LLC
Chambersburg PA
CBHW081801100526
44592CB00015B/2513